GCSE MATHS EXAM TUTOR

INTERMEDIATE TIER

CONTENTS

The accompanying GCSE Maths Exam Tutor CD-ROM for Intermediate Tier is located inside the back cover.

PEARSON
Longman

Pearson Education Limited
Edinburgh Gate
Harlow
Essex
CM20 2JE
England

First published 2003
ISBN 0582 82262 9

Questions, answers, design, typesetting, illustrations and Live Authoring by Live Learning Ltd.

Expert advice by Keith Gordon

Proofreading by Angus Boyd-Heron

Additional typesetting by Derek Lee

Cover design by Raven Design

Printed in the UK by Scotprint, Haddington

The Publisher would like to thank Richard Taylor and John Barrett for their dedication and expertise.

The Publisher's policy is to use paper manufactured from sustainable forests.

INTRODUCTION

Welcome to *GCSE Maths Exam Tutor* for Intermediate Tier – a resource that can be used at home or in class to help you prepare for your exams.

This pack contains:

- two complete sets of sample exam papers and concise answers;
- a CD-ROM with printable sample exam paper PDF files for a variety of specifications.

Each question on the CD-ROM is linked to a worked solution that uses a *Live Player* window – with audio and visual annotation – to guide you through the solution, help you improve exam technique and target the top grades.

Matching your specification

This book contains sample papers written in the style of AQA Specification B Modular exams. However, *Exam Tutor* can be used to support Modular or Linear courses from a variety of awarding bodies. The accompanying CD-ROM (found inside the back cover) contains PDF versions of these exam-style papers for AQA, Edexcel and OCR, Modular and Linear specifications.

You can print off a single copy* of any of these papers and use them like the workbook.

Instructions on how to install and use the CD-ROM are given in the section 'Installation Instructions'.

Using the exam papers in the book

Each paper is similar to ones you will meet in your real exams. On the front page, you are told the module title, whether it is a calculator or non-calculator paper and the amount of time in which you must answer the questions.

Each question has space to show your working and space in which to write your final answer.

Some useful formulae are shown on page 4 of the workbook.

Brief answers are given to all questions in the workbook. These are found at the back of the book.

Using the CD-ROM

You will need to install the *Live Player* software the first time you use the CD-ROM (instructions appear on the next page). Once installation is complete, you can choose the paper you wish to view from the menu screen by clicking on the link for that paper.

When the exam paper appears, you can use Acrobat's back and forward buttons (or previous page and next page buttons) to move between pages.

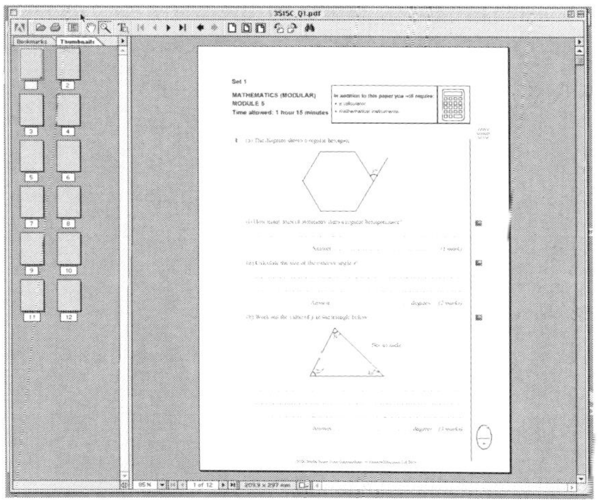

If you wish to see and hear a worked solution, click on the 'LA' icon that appears in the margin of each question paper. This will start the *Live Player* window.

The first time you click on an 'LA' icon a warning message will appear. Tick the option 'do not show this message again' and click 'open' to load the *Live Player* and play the worked solution.

The solution may be paused, replayed or forwarded using the control buttons at the bottom of the *Live Player* window.

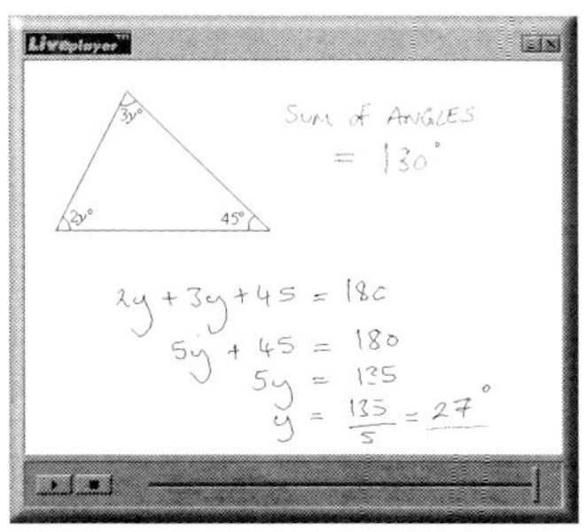

You can also view brief answers for any paper by clicking on the 'Answers' link next to each exam paper link in the menu screen.

* Please note that the User must purchase the Multiple-User Site Licence in order to print off multiple copies of any file from the CD-ROM *or* to use the CD-ROM on more than one computer.

Hardware requirements

Operating system: Windows 95(OS R2), 98, ME, 2000, NT or XP.

Pentium 100 (IBM Compatible PC) or equivalent PC

32 MB RAM or Higher

16 bit graphic card

4 speed CD-ROM drive (minimum 16× recommended)

SVGA colour monitor and 800 × 600 resolution

Sound card

At least 100 MB free hard disk space

Installing the CD-ROM

1 Make sure the CD-ROM is in your CD-ROM drive
2 For Windows 95, 98 and 2000 the installation program starts automatically – go to step 3. If it doesn't, click the START button and click RUN. Enter the drive letter of your CD-ROM drive followed by :\setup (e.g. for a CD-ROM drive configured for letter 'd' type d:\setup). Click OK
3 Follow the instructions on screen

Running GCSE Maths Exam Tutor

1 Make sure the CD-ROM is in your CD-ROM drive
2 Click the Windows START button
3 Click PROGRAMS
4 Click on GCSE Maths Exam Tutor
5 Acrobat Reader should launch and automatically load the Contents page

Note: If you are running the CD-ROM for the first time, when you click on an LA icon in the margin, the *Live Player* will load up to show a worked solution and a dialog box will appear:

1 Click on the option DO NOT SHOW THIS MESSAGE AGAIN
2 Click OPEN and the *Live Player* will load

Uninstalling GCSE Maths Exam Tutor

If at any time you wish to remove this product from your computer please follow these instructions:

1 Click the Windows START button
2 Click SETTINGS
3 Click on CONTROL PANEL
4 Click on ADD/REMOVE PROGRAMS
5 Scroll down the list of programs until you find GCSE Maths Exam Tutor
6 Select the program by clicking on it
7 Click the ADD/REMOVE button
8 Click FINISH when the uninstall program finishes removing the product from your computer

If you receive an error message during installation of Acrobat Reader saying you have the wrong version of Windows Installer please follow these instructions:

For Windows 95 (OS R2), 98 or ME: use Windows Explorer to find the folder called '9598ME' on the CD-ROM. Double-click the folder to open it and double-click on the file called 'InstMsiA.exe'

For Windows 2000 or XP: use Windows Explorer to find the folder called '2000XP' on the CD-ROM. Double-click the folder to open it and double-click on the file called 'InstMsiW.exe'

Follow the on-screen instructions to install the latest version of Windows Installer. Remove and re-insert the CD-ROM to start the GCSE Maths Exam Tutor and Acrobat installation again.

USEFUL FORMULAE

You may need to use the following formulae.

Area of trapezium = $\frac{1}{2}(a + b)h$

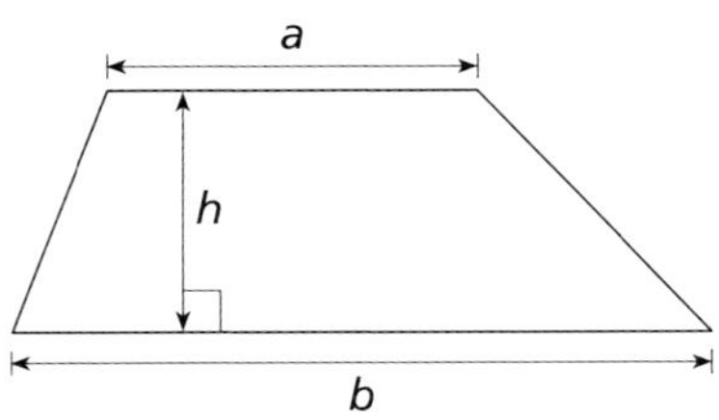

Volume of prism = area of cross section × length

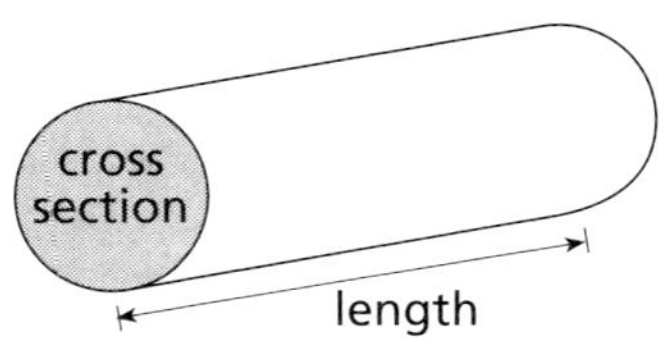

Set 1

MATHEMATICS (MODULAR)
MODULE 1
SECTION A
Time allowed: 25 minutes

In addition to this paper you will require:
- a calculator
- mathematical instruments

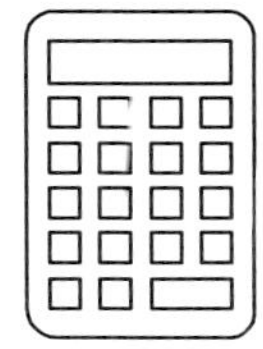

LEAVE MARGIN BLANK

1 A magician has a red bag and a green bag, each containing three cards.

The cards in the red bag are numbered 1, 3 and 5.

The cards in the green bag are numbered 2, 4 and 6.

A member of the audience is invited to take one card at random from each bag.

The numbers on the two cards are added to give a total score.

(a) Show the total score for each possible outcome in the table.

		Card in red bag		
		1	3	5
Card in green bag	2			
	4			
	6			

(2 marks)

(b) What is the probability of getting a total score of 11?

Answer .... *(1 mark)*

(c) What is the probability of getting a total score of **less** than 8?

....

Answer .... *(2 marks)*

5

LEAVE MARGIN BLANK

2 The two-way table shows how the 200 pupils in Year 9 of Waghort's normally travel to school.

	Walk	**Cycle**	**Fly**
Boys	55	18	35
Girls	49	11	32

What is the probability that a pupil chosen at random does not fly to school?

....

....

....

Answer .... *(2 marks)*

2

LEAVE MARGIN BLANK

3 The table shows some data collected in a Biology experiment. The heights of 40 plants were recorded.

Height, *h* cm	**Number of plants**		
$5 \le h < 7$	8		
$7 \le h < 9$	15		
$9 \le h < 11$	12		
$11 \le h < 13$	5		

(a) Use this information to draw a frequency diagram.

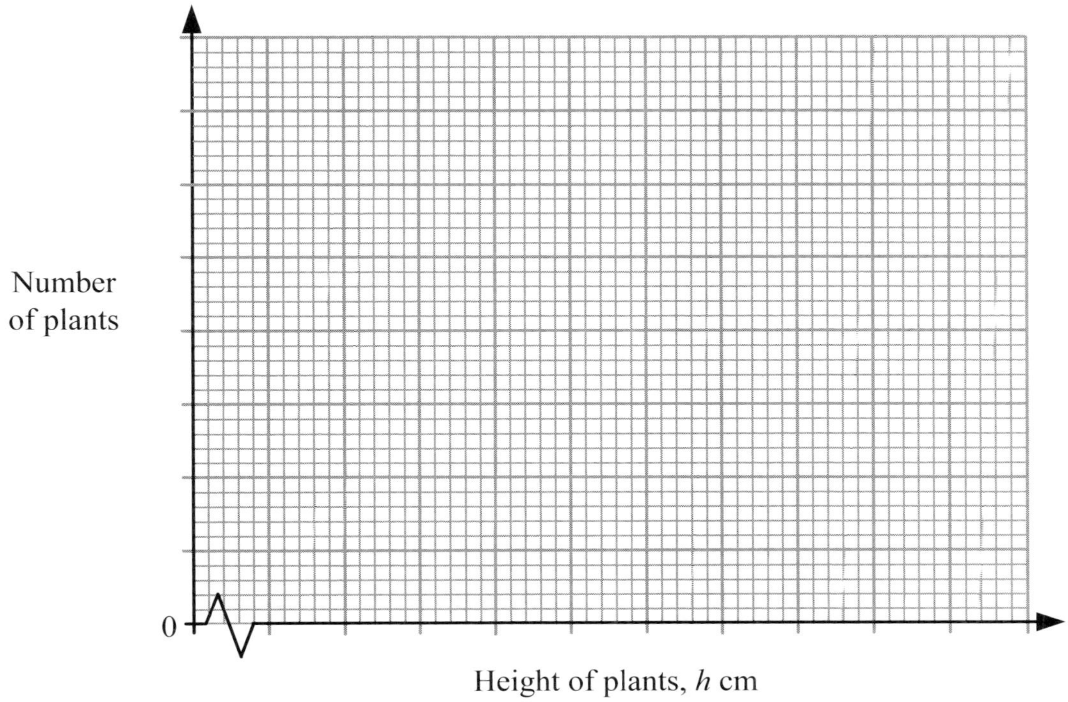

(3 marks)

(b) Calculate an estimate of the mean height of these 40 plants.

....

....

....

....

....

....

Answer .... cm *(4 marks)*

7

4 When Ambrose and Zahir play each other at darts, the probability that Zahir wins is 0.6. A draw is not possible.

Ambrose and Zahir play two games of darts.

(a) Complete and fully label the probability tree diagram to show the possible outcomes.

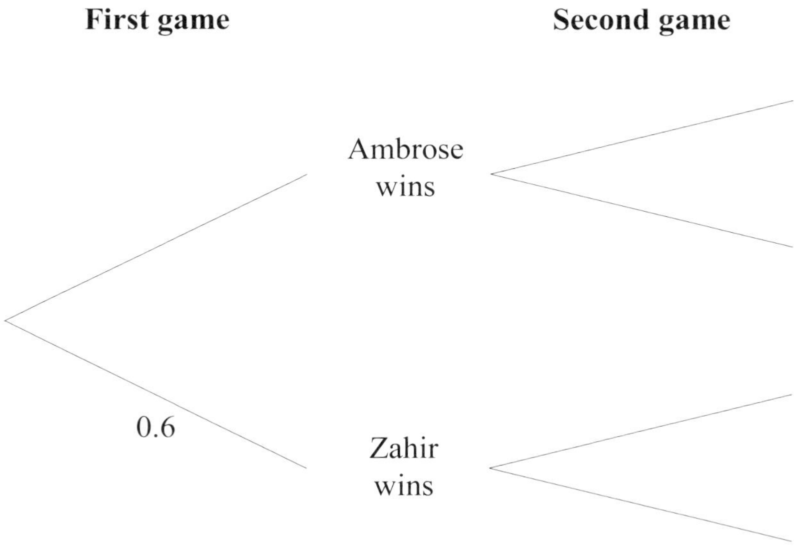

(3 marks)

(b) Calculate the probability that each of them wins only one game.

....

....

....

Answer .... *(2 marks)*

(c) Calculate the probability that Ambrose wins both games.

....

....

Answer .... *(1 mark)*

6

END OF SECTION A

Set 1

MATHEMATICS (MODULAR)
MODULE 1
SECTION B
Time allowed: 25 minutes

In addition to this paper you will require:
- mathematical instruments.

You may **not** use a calculator.

LEAVE MARGIN BLANK

5 For a sponsored charity walk, pupils completed laps of their playing field.

Helen recorded the number of laps completed by pupils in her class in a stem and leaf diagram.

0	8					
1	1	1	6	9	9	
2	2	3	4	7	8	8
3	0	6				
4	2					

Key: | 4 | 2 means 42 laps completed

(a) According to the diagram, how many pupils completed more than 25 laps?

Answer..pupils *(1 mark)*

(b) According to the diagram, what was the median number of laps completed?

....

Answer..laps *(2 marks)*

(c) Later, Helen realised that she had recorded Mary's result twice.

Mary completed 19 laps.

Cross out one of the 19 lap entries from the diagram and find the correct median.

....

Answer..laps *(3 marks)*

6

LEAVE MARGIN BLANK

6 The scatter graph shows the engine sizes in litres of ten types of car made by the Atoyot Motor Company and the cost per mile of running each type of car.

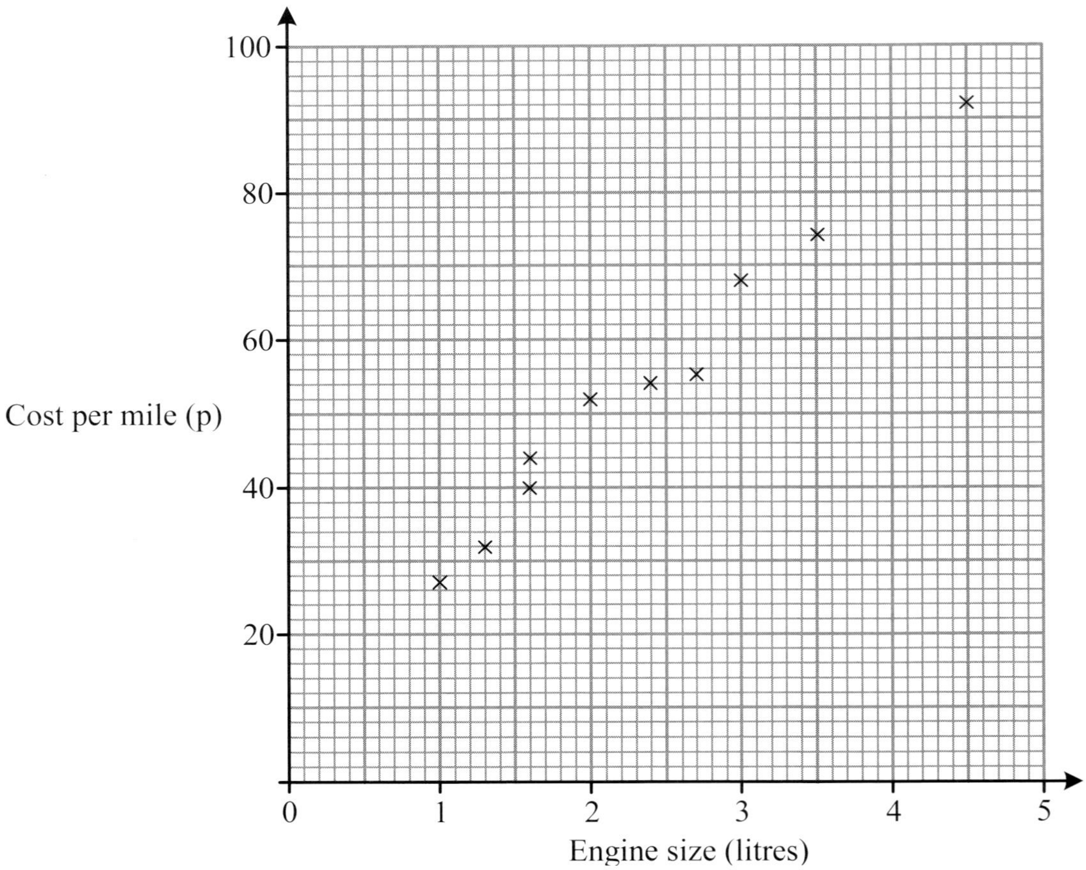

(a) What is the largest size of engine in an Atoyot car that costs less than 50p per mile to run?

Answer..litres *(1 mark)*

(b) Draw a line of best fit on the scatter graph. *(1 mark)*

(c) Describe the relationship shown in the scatter graph.

....

....

(1 mark)

(d) The company plans to produce a small car with an engine size of 0.5 litres.

(i) Estimate the cost per mile of running the car.

Answer..pence *(1 mark)*

(ii) Comment on the reliability of your estimate.

....

....

(1 mark)

5

7 120 pupils took an examination paper. The table gives a summary of their results.

	Marks
Minimum	17
Lower quartile	46
Median	58
Upper quartile	72
Maximum	92

(a) Draw a box plot to show this information.

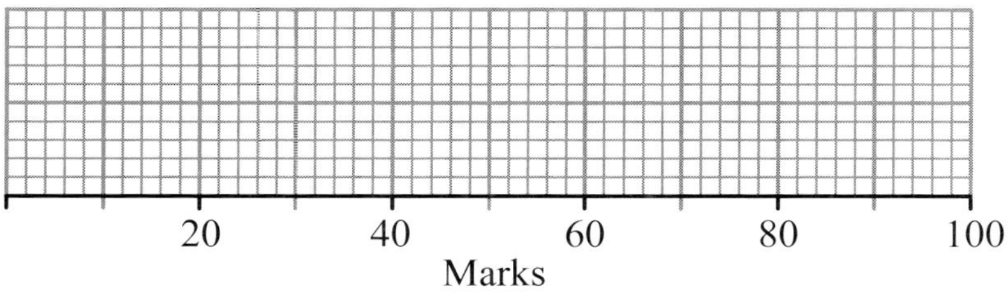

(3 marks)

(b) Write down the interquartile range for these data.

....

Answer.. *(1 mark)*

(c) Estimate how many pupils scored 72 marks or less.

....

Answer.. *(1 mark)*

THIS QUESTION IS CONTINUED ON THE NEXT PAGE

LEAVE MARGIN BLANK

(d) Draw a cumulative frequency diagram to show the information.

The table from the previous page is repeated below.

	Marks
Minimum	17
Lower quartile	46
Median	58
Upper quartile	72
Maximum	92

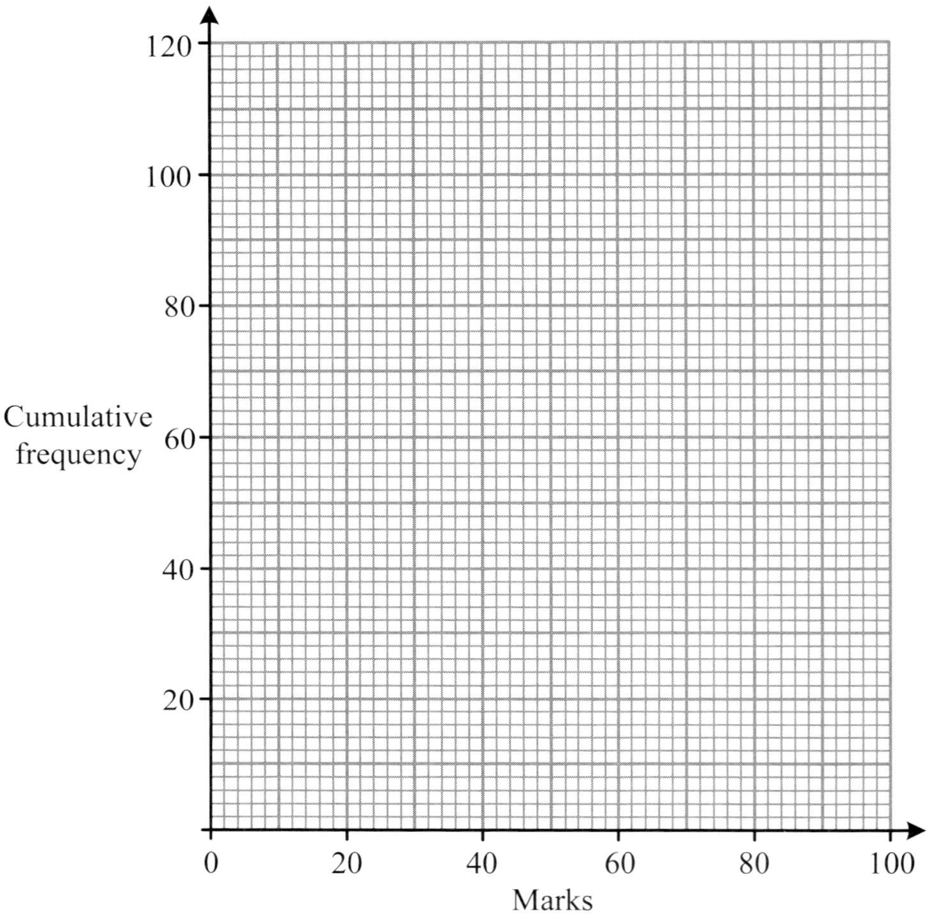

(3 marks)

(e) Grade 1 is awarded to pupils who score 65 marks or more. Use the cumulative frequency diagram to estimate the number of pupils awarded Grade 1.

....

Answer.. *(1 mark)*

9

END OF QUESTIONS

Set 1

MATHEMATICS (MODULAR)
MODULE 3
SECTION A
Time allowed: 40 minutes

In addition to this paper you will require:

- a calculator
- mathematical instruments

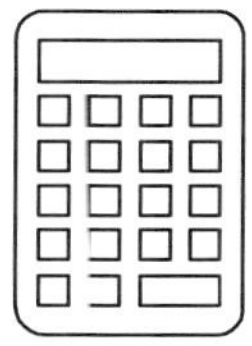

LEAVE MARGIN BLANK

1 On a training run, Harry ran 35 km in 2 hours 30 minutes.

Calculate his average speed.

....

....

....

Answer ....km/h *(3 marks)*

3

2 The total number of spectators at a football match was 17 460.

9730 spectators were City supporters.

What percentage of the spectators were City supporters?

Give your answer to an appropriate degree of accuracy.

....

....

....

....

....

....

Answer ....% *(3 marks)*

3

LEAVE MARGIN BLANK

3 A trader buys 500 videotapes for £250.

He sells all the tapes at a market.

He sells them for £1 each or in packs of 3 for £2.50.

(a) He sells 95 single tapes.

He sells the rest in packs of 3.

How many packs of 3 does he sell?

....

....

....

....

....

....

Answer .... *(2 marks)*

(b) How much money does he receive from selling all the tapes?

....

....

....

....

....

Answer £.. *(2 marks)*

(c) Find the percentage profit made by the trader from the sale of all the tapes.

....

....

....

....

....

Answer ....% *(3 marks)*

7

LEAVE MARGIN BLANK

4 From the following list of numbers

6 13 16 18 21 27 36 40

write down

(a) a cube number

Answer .... *(1 mark)*

(b) a prime number

Answer .... *(1 mark)*

(c) a power of 2

Answer .... *(1 mark)*

3

5 Kyung-Soo buys 8.2 litres of unleaded petrol for £6.15.

The petrol tank of my car holds 38.6 litres.

How much would it cost me to fill the tank of my car with unleaded petrol at the same petrol station?

....

....

....

....

....

Answer £.. *(3 marks)*

3

6 Use your calculator to find the value of $\frac{3.76 \times 0.82}{6.23 - 5.04}$

Give your answer correct to 3 significant figures.

....

....

....

Answer .... *(2 marks)*

2

LEAVE MARGIN BLANK

7 Javagal and Devon share a £35 prize in the ratio 4:3.

How much does Javagal receive?

....

....

....

....

Answer £.. *(3 marks)*

3

8 Light travels 299 800 km in one second.

(a) Write the speed of light in standard form.

....

Answer ....km/s *(1 mark)*

(b) Calculate the distance travelled by light in one minute, giving your answer in standard form.

....

....

....

....

....

Answer ....km *(2 marks)*

3

9 Cans of drink each contain 330 ml correct to the nearest ml.

Calculate the minimum total volume of 6 cans of drink.

....

....

....

Answer ....ml *(2 marks)*

2

LEAVE MARGIN BLANK

10 In a sale, Digipix digital cameras are sold at a discount of 20%.

The sale price of a Digipix camera is £140.

What was the original price of the camera?

....

....

....

....

Answer £.. *(3 marks)*

3

END OF SECTION A

Set 1

MATHEMATICS (MODULAR)
MODULE 3
SECTION B
Time allowed: 40 minutes

In addition to this paper you will require: • mathematical instruments. You may **not** use a calculator.	

LEAVE MARGIN BLANK

11 Roger worked out

$$5^2 - 2^2 = 25 - 4 = 21$$

He then said, 'The difference between any two square numbers is always an odd number.'

Give a counter example to show that Roger is wrong.

....

....

....

(2 marks)

2

12 Tara has a weekend job.

She earns £4.50 per hour on Saturdays.

On Sundays her pay per hour is 50% more than it is on Saturdays.

(a) What is her pay per hour on Sundays?

....

....

....

Answer £.. *(2 marks)*

Last weekend Tara worked for 6 hours on Saturday and for 5 hours on Sunday.

(b) How much did she earn in the two days?

....

....

....

Answer £.. *(3 marks)*

5

LEAVE MARGIN BLANK

13 (a) Write down all the prime numbers between 30 and 40.

....

....

....

Answer .... *(1 mark)*

(b) Find the value of 3×2^3

....

....

Answer .... *(2 marks)*

(c) What is the value of 0.2×0.3?

....

....

Answer .... *(1 mark)*

(d) Work out $\frac{3}{4} - \frac{2}{3}$, giving your answer as a fraction.

....

....

Answer .... *(2 marks)*

6

14 In a sale, a shop sells all its CDs at a discount of 30%.
What is the sale price of a CD that normally costs £12.50?

....

....

....

....

Answer £.. *(3 marks)*

3

LEAVE MARGIN BLANK

15 (a) Find the Least Common Multiple (LCM) of 50 and 75.

....

....

....

....

Answer .... *(2 marks)*

(b) Saturn Bars are sold in two sizes.

A standard bar costs 29p and weighs 50 g. A king-size bar costs 45p and weighs 75 g.

Which size of bar is the better value for money?

....

....

....

....

Answer .... *(2 marks)*

4

16 Express 54 as the product of its prime factors.

....

....

....

....

....

Answer .... *(3 marks)*

3

LEAVE MARGIN BLANK

17 You are given that $7.6 \times 13.2 = 100.32$ exactly.

(a) Justine says that $76 \times 0.0132 = 10.032$.

Without doing an exact calculation, show that Justine is wrong.

....

....

....

....

(2 marks)

(b) Find the exact value of 0.076×132.

....

....

....

Answer .... *(2 marks)*

4

18 (a) Find an approximate value for $8.96 \div 0.321$

You **must** show all your working.

....

....

....

Answer .... *(2 marks)*

(b) Find an approximate value for $\dfrac{3.125 \times 10^5}{4.937 \times 10^{-3}}$

Give your answer in standard form.

....

....

....

....

Answer .... *(3 marks)*

5

END OF QUESTIONS

Set 1

MATHEMATICS (MODULAR)
MODULE 5
Time allowed: 1 hour 15 minutes

In addition to this paper you will require:
- mathematical instruments.

You may **not** use a calculator.

LEAVE MARGIN BLANK

1 Write these numbers in order of size, starting with the smallest:

$$\frac{2}{3}, \quad 0.6, \quad \frac{5}{8}, \quad 0.607$$

....

....

Answer .... *(2 marks)* 2

2 The diagram shows triangle *ABC*.

Angle *ABC* is a right angle and angle *BCA* = 36°.

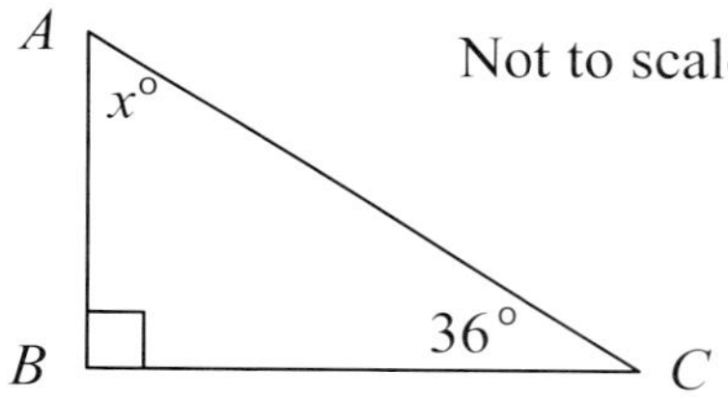

Not to scale

Work out the value of x.

Give a reason for your answer.

....

Answer x = ... degrees

Reason ....

....

(2 marks) 2

LEAVE MARGIN BLANK

3 David has a fish tank, which is a cuboid of length 50 cm, width 30 cm and height 24 cm.

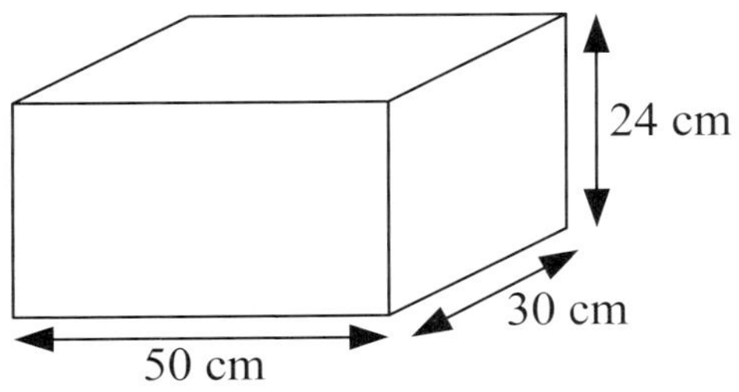

(a) Find the volume of David's fish tank.

....

....

....

Answer .... cm^3 *(2 marks)*

The volume of Gemma's tank is two thirds of the volume of David's tank.

(b) Find the volume of Gemma's tank.

....

....

....

Answer .... cm^3 *(2 marks)*

4

4 When you input a number into a 'number machine', the machine subtracts 6 from the number and then divides the result by 3.

The result is then output.

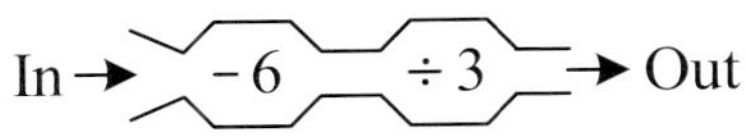

(a) If the input is 15, what is the output?

....

....

Answer .... *(1 mark)*

(b) If the output is 7, what is the input?

....

....

Answer .... *(2 marks)*

3

LEAVE MARGIN BLANK

5 The map, which is drawn to scale, shows three towns, Axton, Bixton and Coxton. The towns are joined by straight roads.

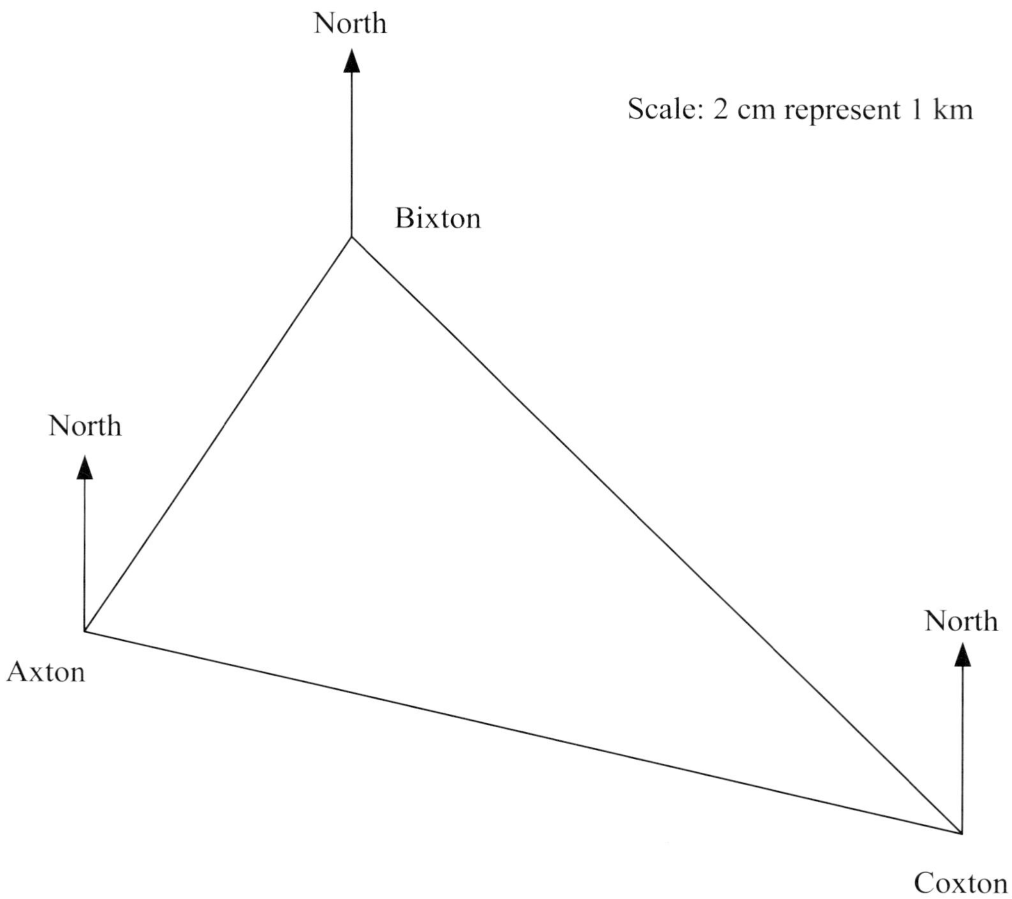

(a) Measure and write down the three-figure bearing of Bixton from Axton.

Answer ....° *(1 mark)*

(b) Measure and write down the three-figure bearing of Bixton from Coxton.

....

Answer .... ° *(1 mark)*

(c) A new straight road is to be built from Bixton on a bearing of 165°. Draw this road on the diagram as far as the point at which it reaches the road between Axton and Coxton.

(2 marks)

(d) A village, Duffield, is 2 km due west of Bixton. Mark the position of Duffield with a cross on the diagram.

(2 marks)

6

6 The graph shows Rosa's journey to visit her grandparents.

She is driven from home to the railway station by her mother. She waits for a train.

She then travels by train and her grandparents meet her at the end of her journey.

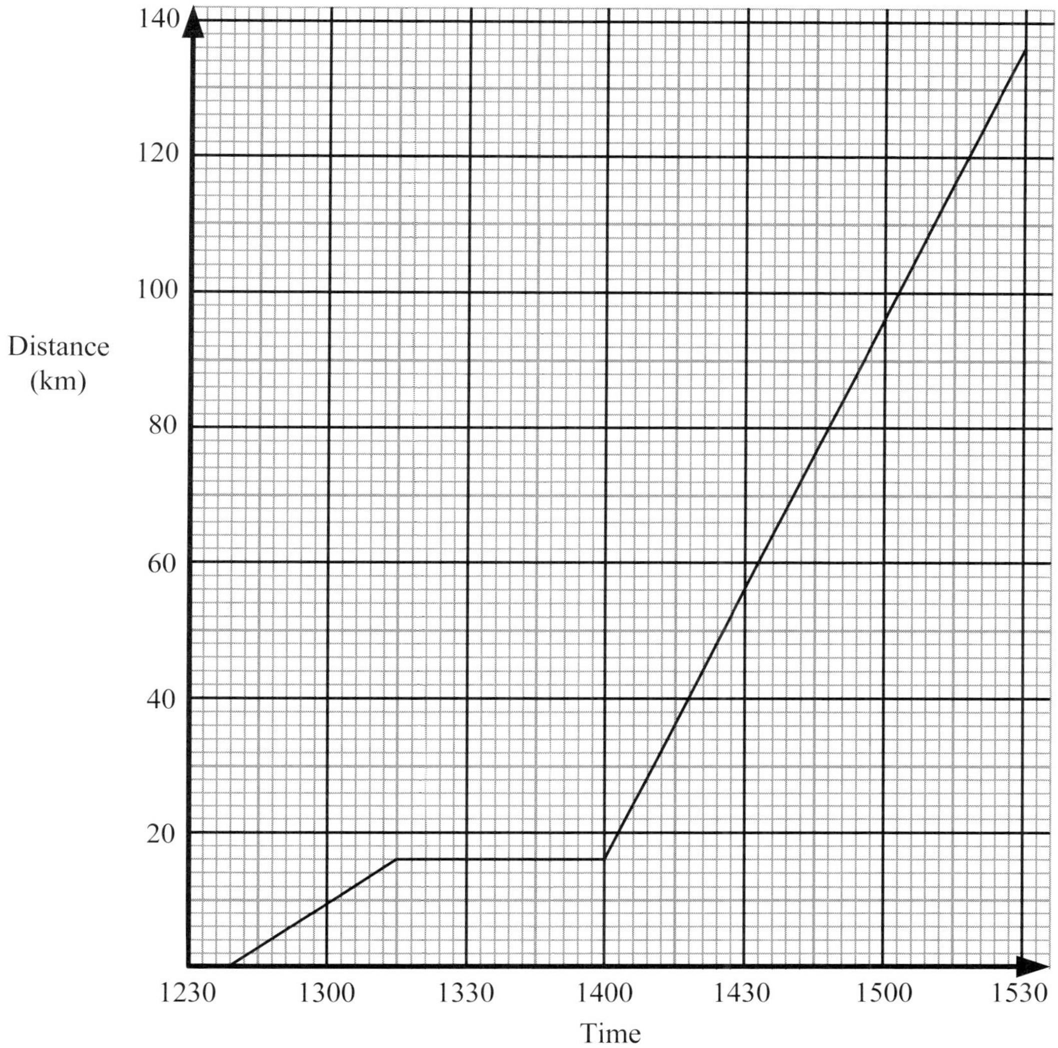

(a) How far is the station from Rosa's home?

Answer .... km *(1 mark)*

(b) For how many minutes does Rosa wait for the train?

....

Answer .... minutes *(1 mark)*

(c) Calculate the average speed of the train in kilometres per hour.

....

....

....

Answer .... km/h *(3 marks)*

5

LEAVE MARGIN BLANK

7 The diagram shows a trapezium.

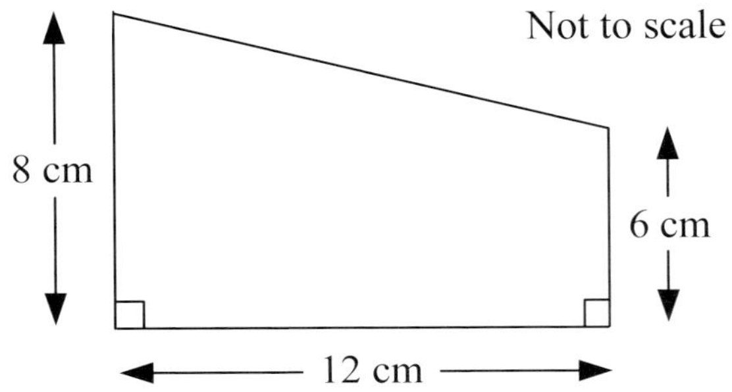

Calculate the area of the trapezium.

....

....

....

Answer ....cm^2 *(2 marks)*

2

8 (a) Write down the first three terms of the sequence whose nth term is $n^2 + 3$.

....

....

Answer .... *(2 marks)*

(b) What is the 20th term of the sequence?

....

....

Answer .... *(1 mark)*

(c) What is the nth term of the sequence whose first five terms are 6, 9, 14, 21, 30?

....

....

Answer .... *(1 mark)*

4

LEAVE MARGIN BLANK

9 The diagram shows an isometric representation of a house.

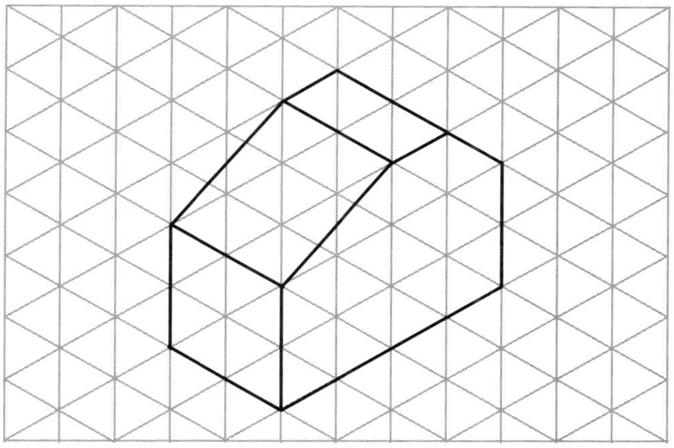

On the grid below, draw the plan of the house.

The plan is the view from above the house.

(2 marks)

2

LEAVE MARGIN BLANK

10 (a) Factorise

$$x^2 - 3x$$

....

Answer .... *(1 mark)*

(b) Solve the equation, giving your answer as a fraction.

$$3x - 2 = 8$$

....

....

Answer .... *(2 marks)*

(c) Solve the equation

$$4(x - 3) = 3x + 10$$

....

....

....

....

Answer .... *(3 marks)*

/ 6

LEAVE MARGIN BLANK

11 (a) Complete the table of values for $y = 6 + 2x - x^2$ and use it to draw the graph of $y = 6 + 2x - x^2$ for values of x from –3 to 4.

x	–3	–2	–1	0	1	2	3	4
y		–2	3	6		6	3	–2

(2 marks)

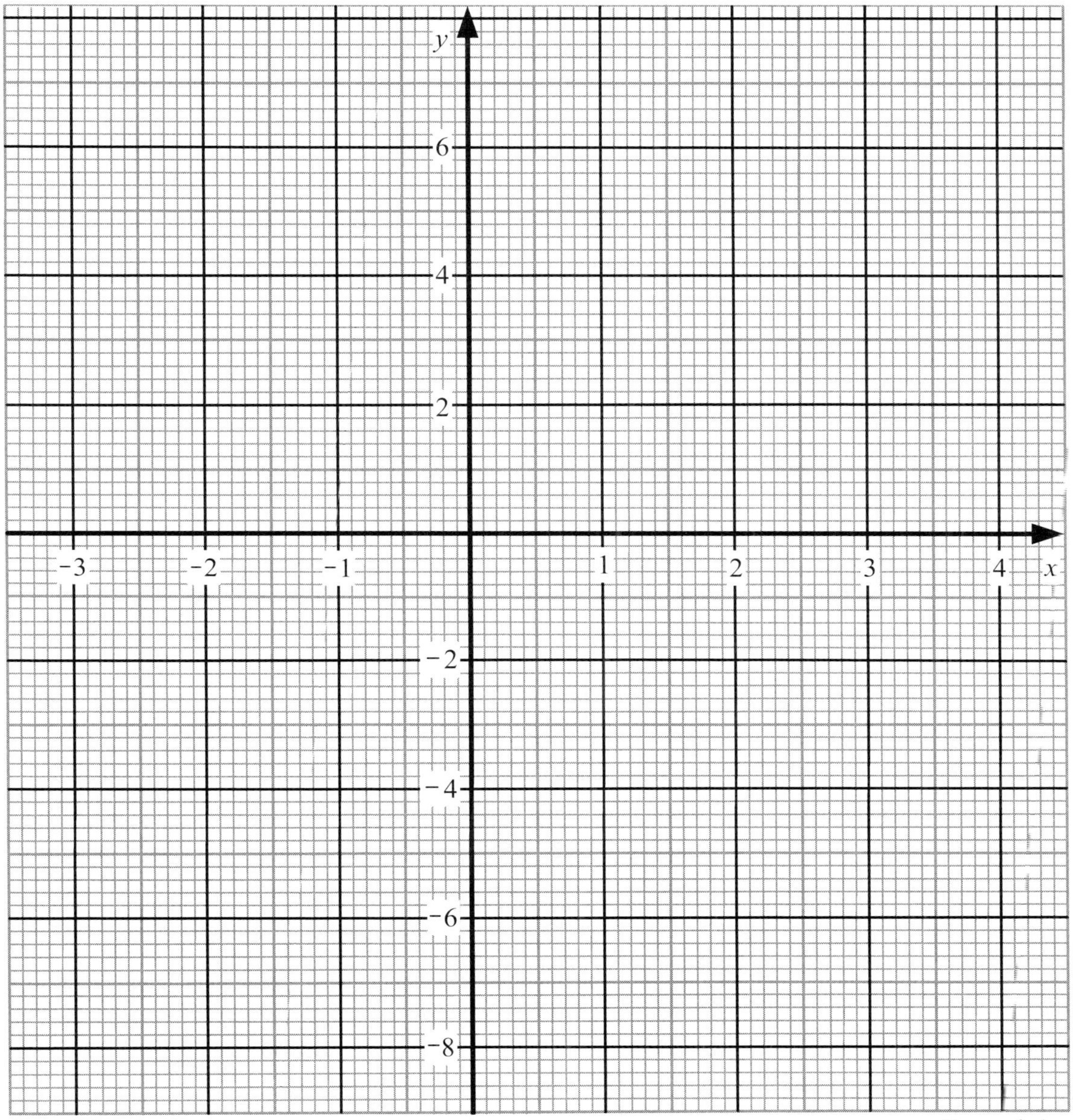

(2 marks)

(b) On the same axes, draw the graph of the line $y = x + 3$.

....

.... *(2 marks)*

(c) Write down, correct to one decimal place, the coordinates of the point with a positive x coordinate where the line meets the curve.

Answer (.............. , ...) *(1 mark)*

7

12 A is the point (12, 12), B is the point (4, 10) and C is the point (6, 6).

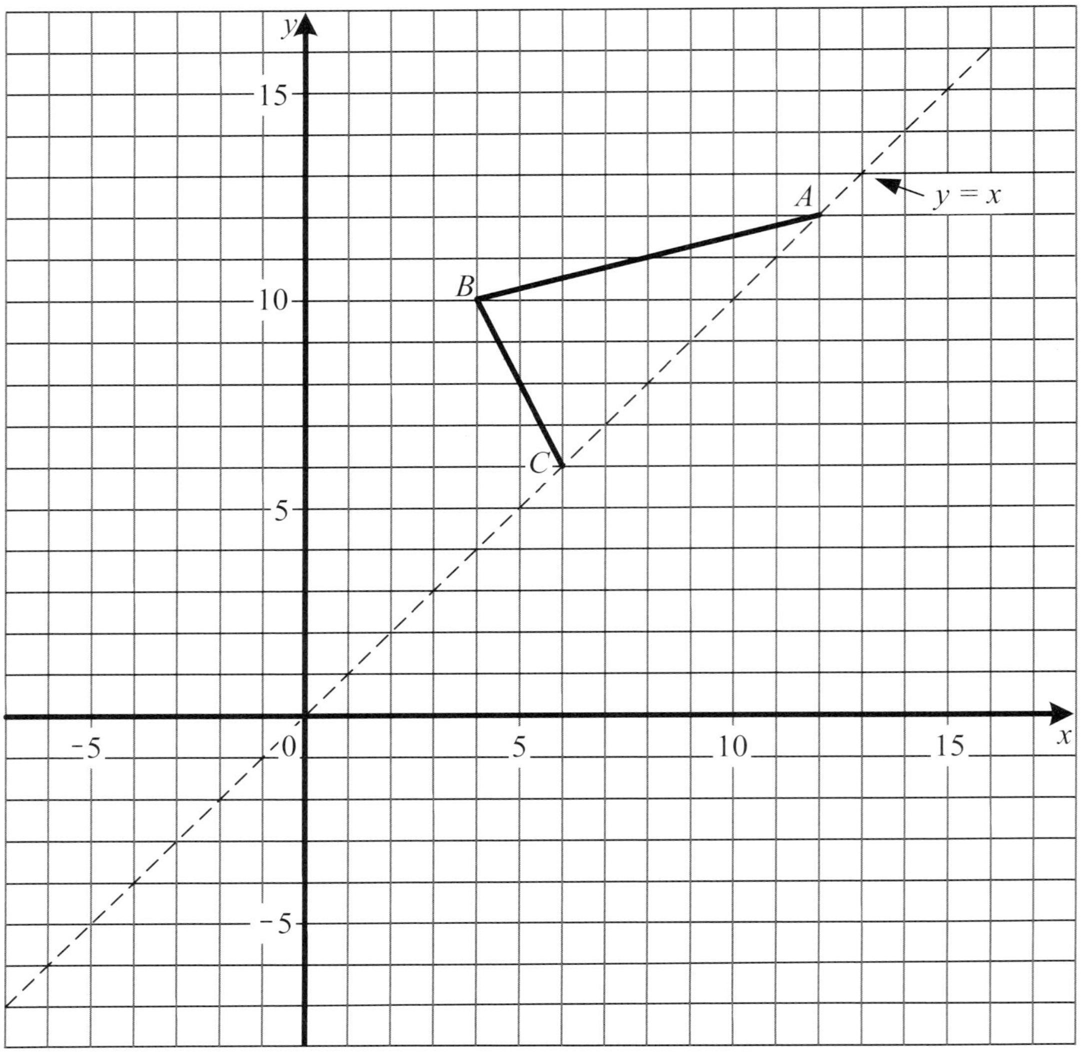

AB and BC are two sides of a quadrilateral $ABCD$ which has the line $y = x$ as a line of symmetry.

(a) On the diagram, draw the sides CD and AD of the quadrilateral, and write down the coordinates of D.

Answer (.............. , ...) *(2 marks)*

$ABCD$ is enlarged by a scale factor of $\frac{1}{2}$, with the origin as the centre of enlargement, to produce the figure $A'B'C'D'$.

(b) On the diagram, draw $A'B'C'D'$.

(3 marks)

5

LEAVE MARGIN BLANK

13 Peter wants to plant a tree in his garden.

The garden is drawn to scale below. The line *AD* represents the outside wall of Peter's house.

The tree must be closer to the wall *AB* than to the house.

It must also be closer to *C* than to *D*.

On the diagram, shade the area in which the tree may be planted.

All your construction lines must be shown clearly.

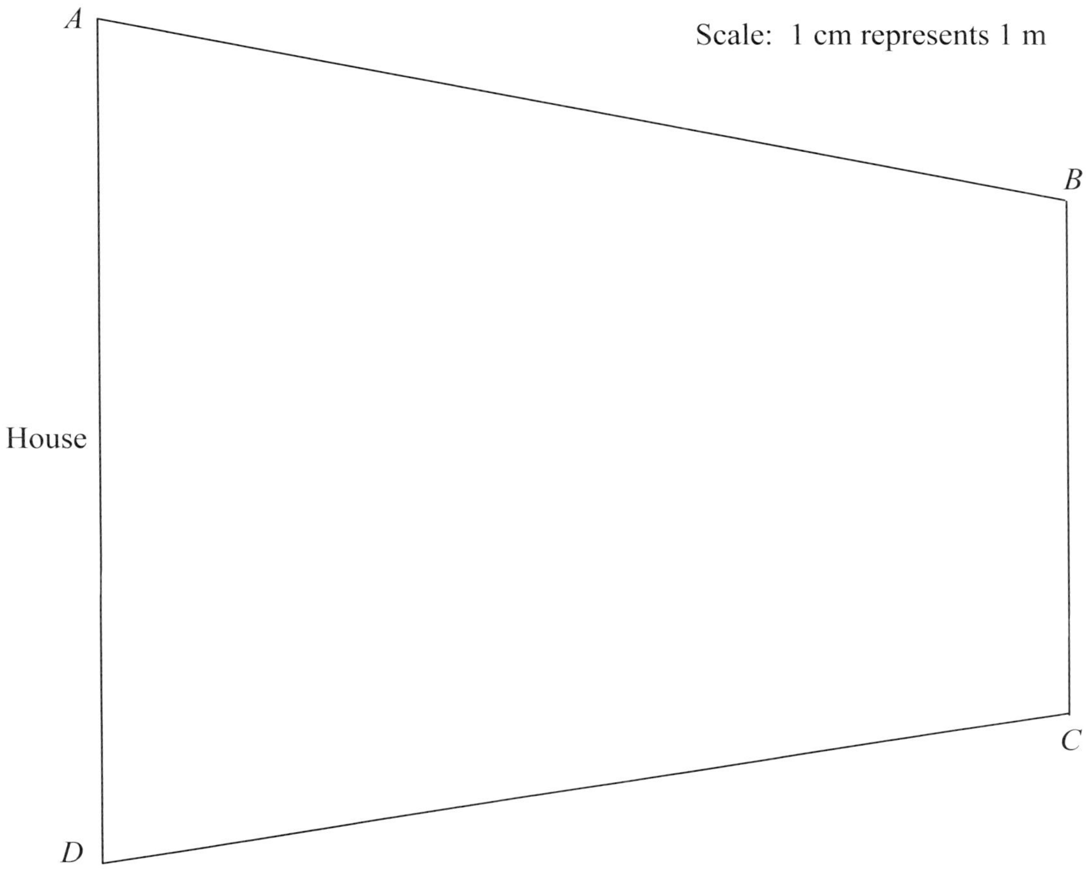

(4 marks)

4

14 In the diagram, AB is a diameter of the circle and O is the centre of the circle.
Angle $BAC = 73°$.

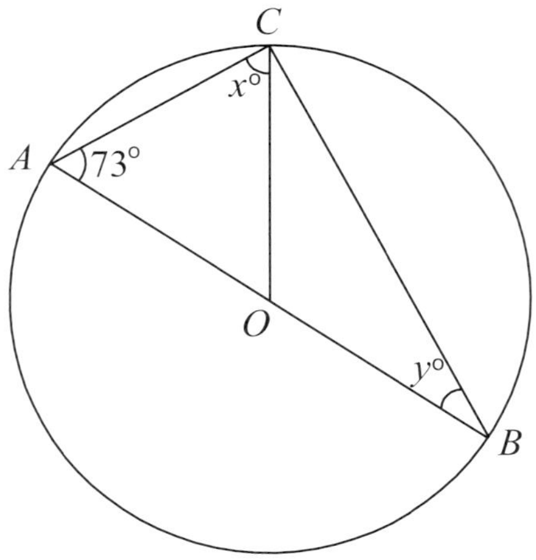

Not to scale

(a) Calculate the value of x, giving a reason for your answer.

....

....

Answer ....° *(2 marks)*

(b) Calculate the value of y, giving a reason for your answer.

....

....

Answer ....° *(2 marks)*

4

15 Rupert is using the formula $A = \pi x(y + z)$ to calculate an area.

He knows that x, y and z are all lengths measured in cm.

Becky says, 'You shouldn't be using that formula to calculate an area. It hasn't got any squares in it.'

Is Becky correct?

Explain your answer.

....

....

....

(2 marks)

2

LEAVE MARGIN BLANK

16 Below are four equations:

Equation 1: $y = 2x - 3$

Equation 2: $y = x^2 - 3$

Equation 3: $3x + 5y = 15$

Equation 4: $y = 2x^3$

(a) Match one of the equations to each of the three graphs below.

Graph A

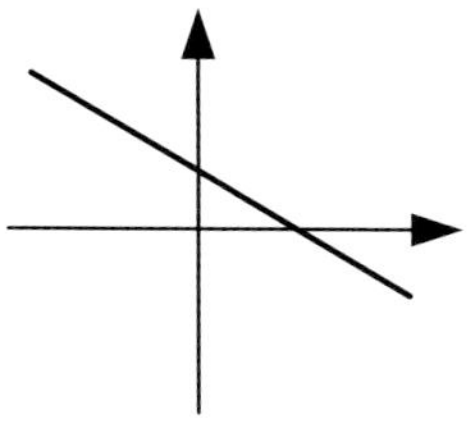

Equation ....

Graph B

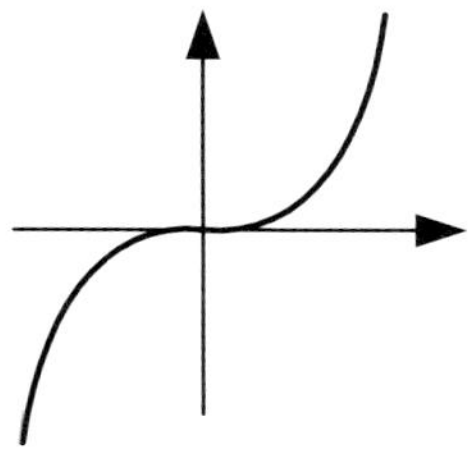

Equation ....

Graph C

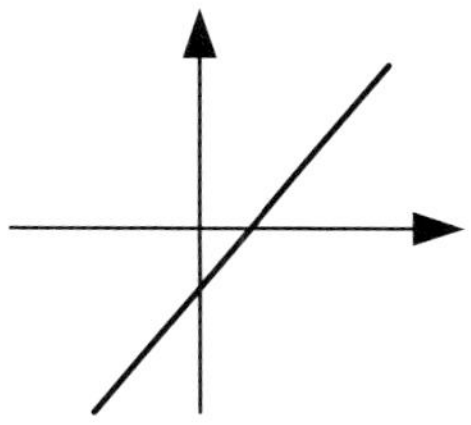

Equation ....

(3 marks)

(b) Draw the graph of the remaining equation on the axes below.

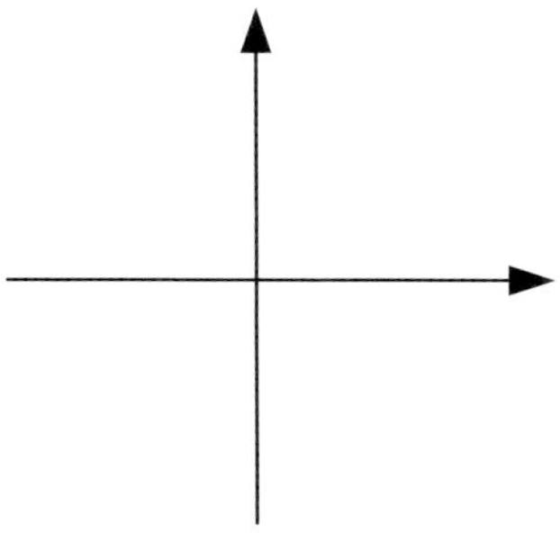

(2 marks)

5

LEAVE MARGIN BLANK

17 (a) (i) Factorise $x^2 - 5x + 6$

....

....

....

....

Answer .... *(3 marks)*

(ii) Solve the equation $x^2 - 5x + 6 = 0$

....

....

Answer .... *(1 mark)*

(b) Solve the simultaneous equations

$$2x - y = 12$$
$$3x + 4y = 7$$

....

....

....

....

....

Answer .... *(3 marks)*

7

END OF QUESTIONS

Set 1

MATHEMATICS (MODULAR)
MODULE 5
Time allowed: 1 hour 15 minutes

In addition to this paper you will require:
- a calculator
- mathematical instruments

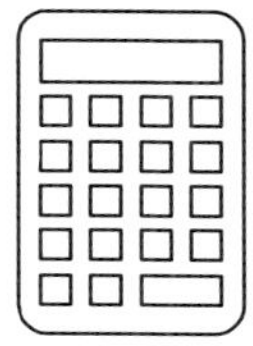

LEAVE MARGIN BLANK

1 (a) The diagram shows a regular hexagon.

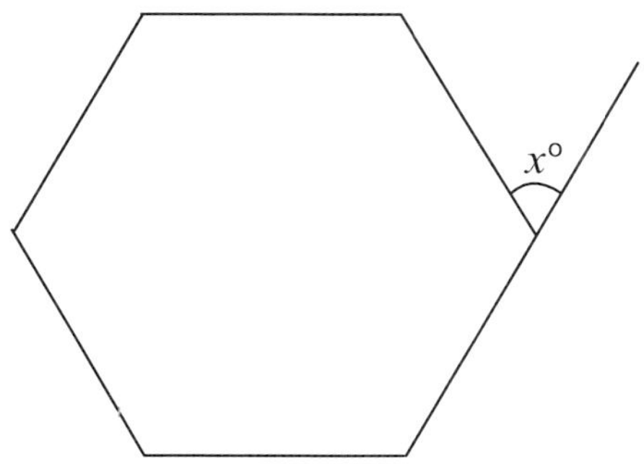

(i) How many axes of symmetry does a regular hexagon have?

....

Answer .... *(1 mark)*

(ii) Calculate the size of the exterior angle $x°$.

....

....

Answer .... degrees *(2 marks)*

(b) Work out the value of y in the triangle below.

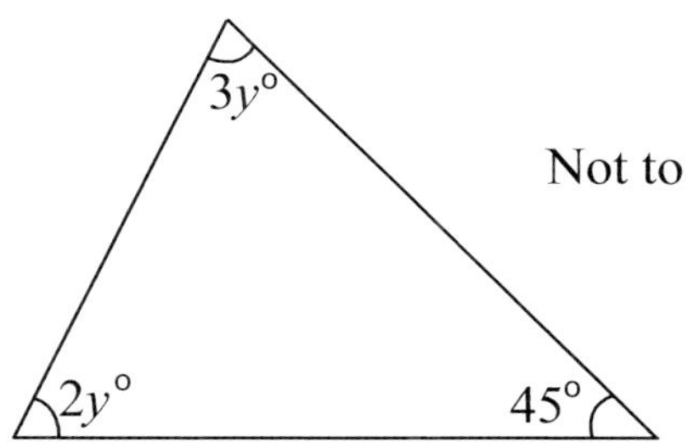

Not to scale

....

....

....

Answer .... degrees *(3 marks)*

6

LEAVE MARGIN BLANK

2 Below are four mathematical expressions

$$\mathbf{2(n-3)} \qquad \mathbf{n^2-3} \qquad \mathbf{\frac{n-3}{2}} \qquad \mathbf{2n-3}$$

(a) Match the expression with the appropriate description.

Peter has n marbles in a bag.

(i) Paul had twice as many marbles as Peter.

He gave 3 to his brother.

Paul now has .... marbles.

(ii) Mary had three marbles less than Peter to start with.

After playing a game she doubled the number of marbles that she had.

Mary now has .... marbles.

(iii) Simon had n bags each containing n marbles.

He lost 3 marbles down a drain.

Simon now has .... marbles.

(3 marks)

(b) Write a description that describes the remaining expression. Your description should end with 'Garfunkel now has .... marbles'.

....

....

....

....

Garfunkel now has .... marbles. *(1 mark)*

4

LEAVE MARGIN BLANK

3 (a) Solve the inequality $4x > x - 9$

....

....

....

Answer .... *(2 marks)*

(b) Multiply out and simplify $(2x - 1)(x + 3)$

....

....

Answer .... *(2 marks)*

(c) Simplify $3x^4 \times 2x^2$

....

....

Answer .... *(2 marks)*

(d) Simplify $\frac{x}{2} \times \frac{2x}{3}$

....

....

Answer .... *(2 marks)*

$\overline{\quad 8}$

LEAVE MARGIN BLANK

4 Emily is using trial and improvement to find a solution of the equation $x^3 - 5x = 30$.

The table shows her first two trials.

x	$x^3 - 5x$	**Comment**
3	12	Too small
4	44	Too large

Continue the table to find a solution of the equation.

Give your answer correct to **1 decimal place**.

Answer $x =$ .... *(3 marks)*

3

5 (a) Solve the equation

$$2x - 2 = 5$$

....

....

....

Answer .... *(2 marks)*

(b) Rearrange the formula

$$2Q - P = S$$

to make Q the subject.

....

....

....

....

Answer .... *(2 marks)*

4

LEAVE MARGIN BLANK

6 (a) Work out $\frac{8.4}{1.6 \times 2.8}$

....

....

Answer .... *(2 marks)*

(b) If $a = -6$ and $b = 14$, find the value of

(i) $3a + b$

....

....

Answer .... *(2 marks)*

(ii) $b^2 - a^2$

....

....

Answer .... *(2 marks)*

(iii) $\frac{a}{a - b}$

....

....

Answer .... *(2 marks)*

8

LEAVE MARGIN BLANK

7 In triangle ABC, angle ABC is a right angle, $AC = 5.3$ cm and $BC = 4.7$ cm.

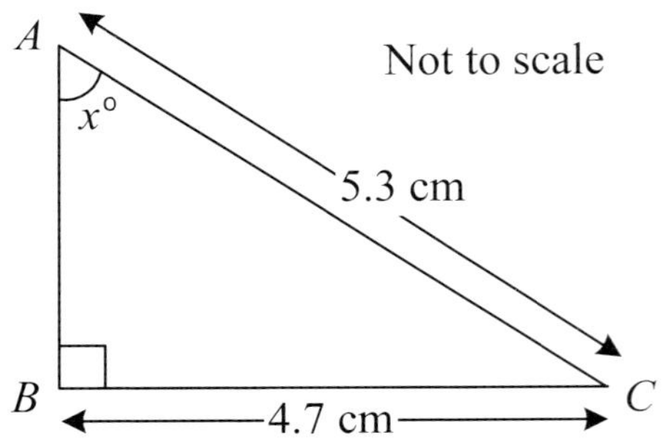

(a) Calculate the length of AB.

....

....

....

....

Answer .... cm *(3 marks)*

(b) Calculate the value of x.

....

....

....

....

Answer .... ° *(3 marks)*

6

LEAVE MARGIN BLANK

8 Part of a number grid is shown below.

1	2	3	4	5	6	7	8	9	10
11	12	13	14	15	15	17	18	19	20
21	22	23	24	25	26	27	28	29	30
31	32	33	34	35	36	37	38	39	40
41	42	43	44	45	46	47	48	49	50

The shaded shape is called T_{14}, because 14 is the number at the centre of the top row of the 'T'.

The sum of the numbers in T_{14} is 100.

(a) Fill in the empty squares of T_n.

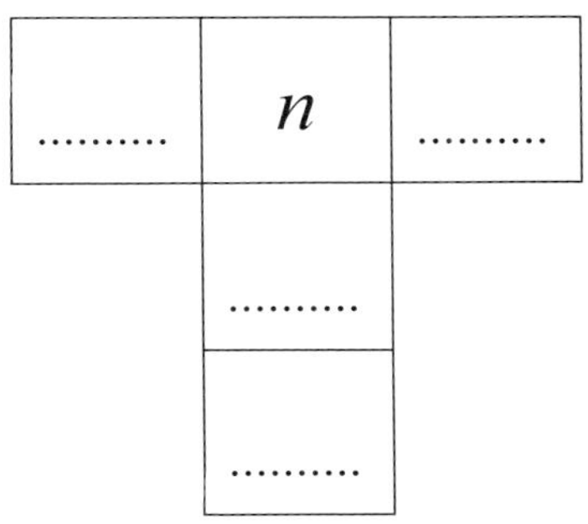

(3 marks)

(b) Find the sum of all the numbers in T_n, in terms of n.

Give your answer in its simplest form.

....

....

....

Answer .... *(2 marks)*

(c) Explain why you cannot find a shape T_n for which the sum of the numbers is 236.

....

....

....

....

(2 marks)

7

LEAVE MARGIN BLANK

9 The recommended cooking time for roast meat is 20 minutes for every 500 g, plus 20 minutes.

(a) Angela has a piece of meat weighing 1.5 kg that she wants to roast. For how long should she cook the meat?

....

....

....

Answer .... minutes *(2 marks)*

(b) Brian has a piece of meat that he wants to roast.

He calculates that he will need to cook it for 110 minutes.

What is the weight of Brian's piece of meat?

....

....

....

....

....

Answer ....kg *(2 marks)*

(c) Using W kg for the weight of a piece of meat and T minutes for the time needed to roast it, write down a formula for T in terms of W.

....

....

....

....

Answer .... *(2 marks)*

6

LEAVE MARGIN BLANK

10

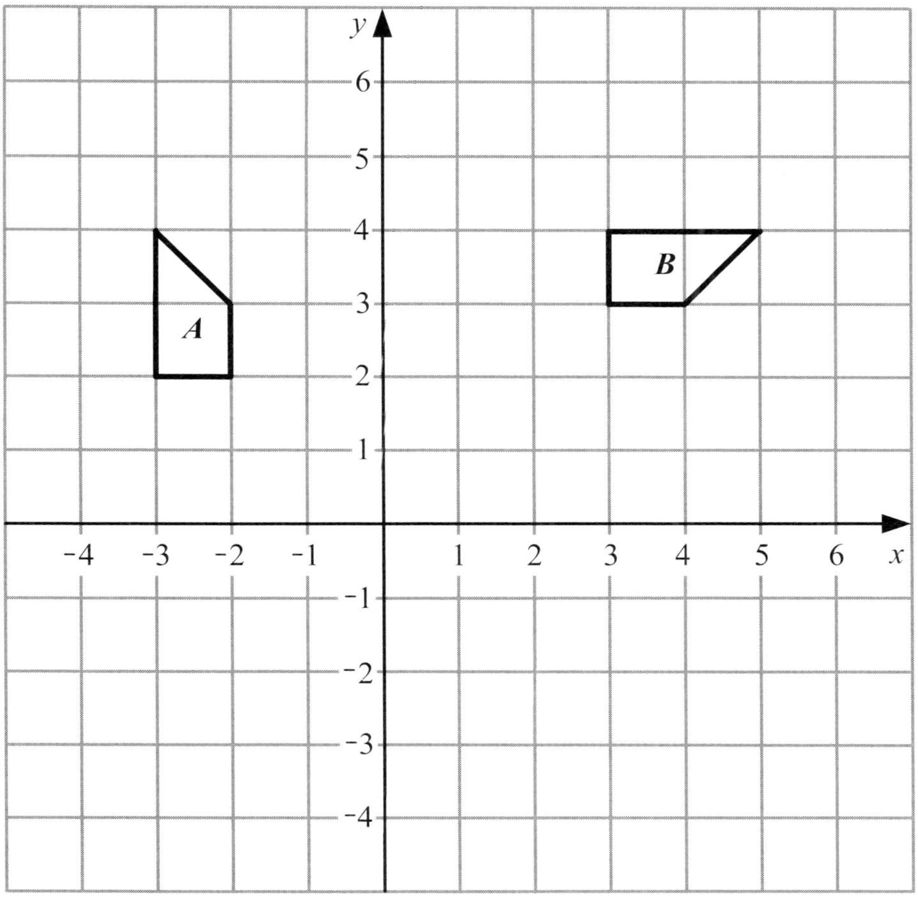

(a) On the diagram, draw the image of Shape ***A*** when it is reflected in the x-axis.

(1 mark)

(b) On the diagram, draw the image of Shape ***B*** when it is translated by the vector $\begin{pmatrix} 1 \\ -2 \end{pmatrix}$.

(1 mark)

(c) Describe fully the single transformation which will map Shape ***A*** onto Shape ***B***.

....

....

....

(3 marks)

5

LEAVE MARGIN BLANK

11 A drinking glass is made in the shape of a cylinder which is open at one end.

The radius of the cylinder is r cm and its height is h cm.

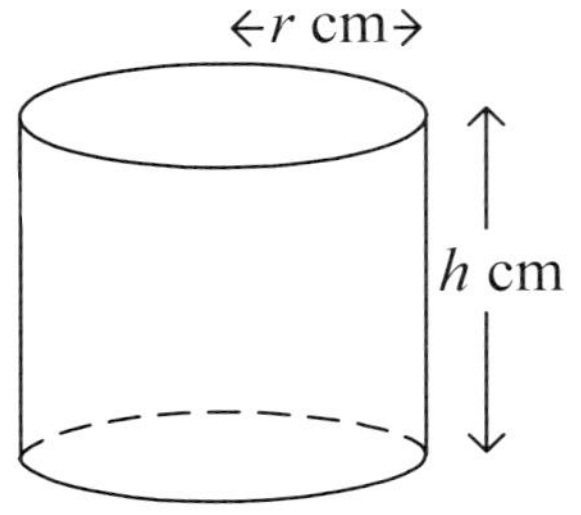

(a) If the surface area of the outside of the glass is A cm^2, show that

$$A = \pi r^2 + 2\pi rh.$$

....

....

....

....

....

....

Answer .... *(2 marks)*

(b) Calculate the value of A if $r = 3$ and $h = 10$.

....

....

....

Answer .... cm^2 *(1 mark)*

3

LEAVE MARGIN BLANK

12 (a) Asif measures the length of his foot. He writes the result down as

24 cm, correct to the nearest centimetre

Write down the smallest possible length of his foot.

....

Answer .... cm *(1 mark)*

(b) Bashir measures his foot. He writes down the result of his measurement as

23.5 cm, correct to the nearest half centimetre

Write down the greatest possible length of his foot.

....

Answer .... cm *(1 mark)*

(c) Clive looks at these results and says, 'Asif's foot is longer than Bashir's'.

Bashir says, 'You can't be sure about that. You need to measure more accurately.'

Is Bashir right?

Answer ....

Give a reason for your answer.

Reason ....

....

....

....

(2 marks)

4

LEAVE MARGIN BLANK

13 *ABCD* is a parallelogram.

AB is 6 cm long and *BC* is 10 cm long.

(a) Make an accurate drawing of the parallelogram in the space below.

Sides *AB* and *BC* have been drawn for you.

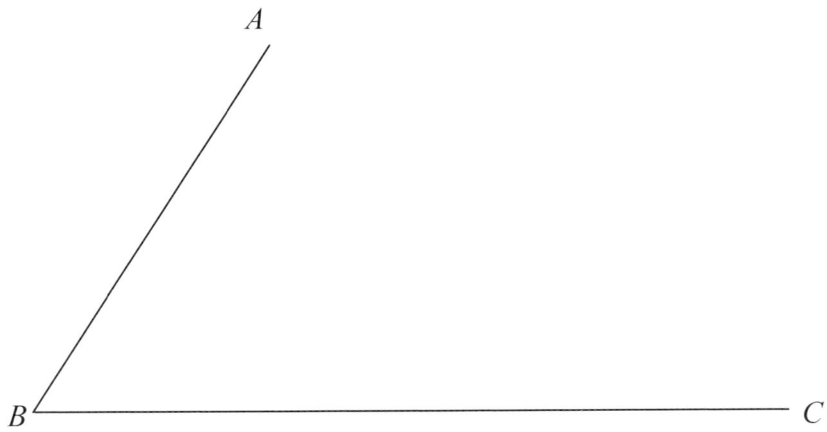

(2 marks)

(b) The point *P* is the foot of the perpendicular from *A* to *BC*.

Construct the line *AP*.

(2 marks)

(c) Calculate the area of the parallelogram *ABCD*.

....

....

....

Answer .... cm^2 *(2 marks)*

6

END OF QUESTIONS

Set 2

MATHEMATICS (MODULAR)
MODULE 1
SECTION A
Time allowed: 25 minutes

In addition to this paper you will require:
- a calculator
- mathematical instruments

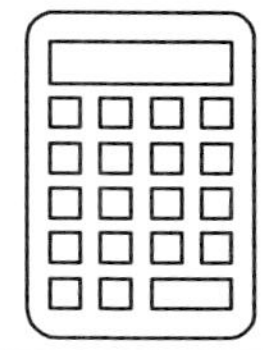

LEAVE MARGIN BLANK

1 In a game, a blue spinner and a yellow spinner are spun.

Both spinners are fair and are numbered 0, 1, 2, 4.
The numbers on the two spinners are multiplied together to produce a score.

(a) Complete the table to show all the possible scores.

Blue spinner

Yellow spinner		0	1	2	4
	0				
	1			2	
	2	0			8
	4				

(2 marks)

(b) What is the probability of getting a score of 1?

Answer .... *(1 mark)*

(c) What is the probability of getting a score of more than 4?

Answer .... *(2 marks)*

5

2 Serena and Venus play a game of cards.

They have played 150 times before.
15 of their games were drawn.

(a) Estimate the probability that their next game will be drawn.

....

Answer .... *(1 mark)*

Serena is twice as likely to win as Venus.

(b) What is the probability that Venus wins?

....

....

Answer .... *(2 marks)*

3

LEAVE MARGIN BLANK

3 Philippe conducted a survey among schoolchildren outside his town's swimming pool.

The two-way table shows the results of his survey.

	Can swim	**Cannot swim**
Boys	35	18
Girls	19	8

1743 children go to school in the town.

(a) Use the results of the survey to estimate the number of schoolchildren in the town who can swim.

Give your answer to a suitable degree of accuracy.

....

....

....

....

....

....

Answer .... *(4 marks)*

(b) Give a reason why Philippe's sample may not be representative.

....

....

....

(1 mark)

5

LEAVE MARGIN BLANK

4 The table shows the amount paid by a company for the water supplied to it.

Date of bill	Jan 2001	Apr 2001	July 2001	Oct 2001	Jan 2002	Apr 2002	July 2002	Oct 2002
Amount (£)	40	58	112	190	54	60	130	200

The time series graph shows these data.

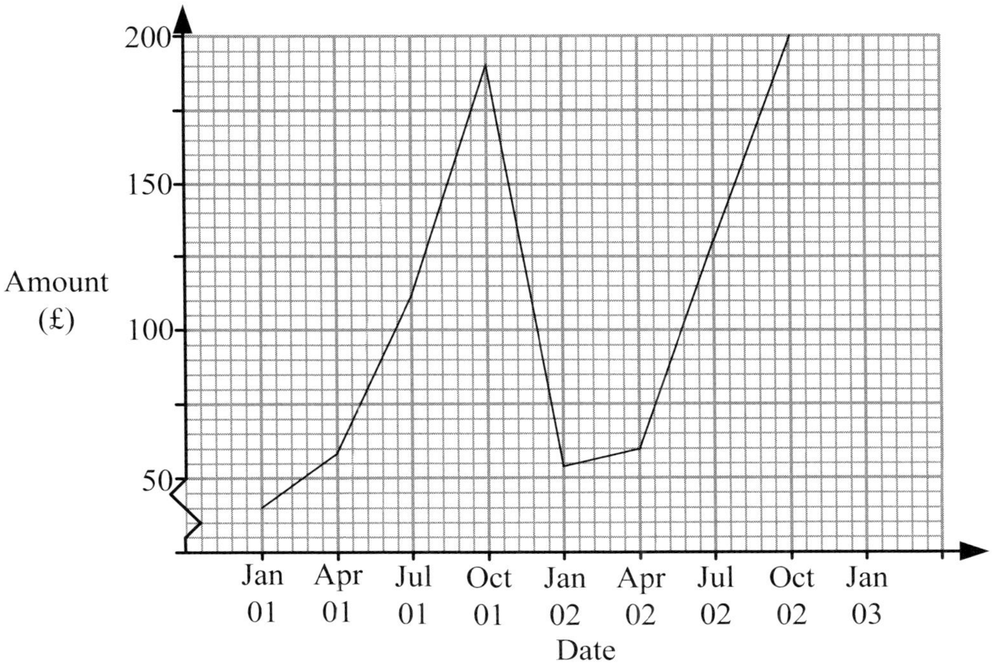

(a) Calculate the first value of the four-point moving average for the data.

....

....

Answer £... *(2 marks)*

The remaining values of the four-point moving average are: 103.5, 104, 108.5, 111

(b) Plot all five values of the moving average on the graph.

(2 marks)

(c) Using a trend line, or otherwise, estimate the four-point moving average for the next period, April 2002 to January 2003.

Answer £... *(1 mark)*

(d) Use the value from part (c) to calculate a prediction of the amount the company will have to pay for water in January 2003.

....

....

Answer £... *(2 marks)*

END OF SECTION A

7

Set 2

MATHEMATICS (MODULAR)
MODULE 1
SECTION B
Time allowed: 25 minutes

In addition to this paper you will require:
- mathematical instruments.

You may **not** use a calculator.

LEAVE MARGIN BLANK

5 The Pizza Parlour sells four types of basic pizza.

Ravi is a waiter at the Pizza Parlour.
He keeps a record of the number of each type of pizza that he serves.
The table below shows the numbers for one day.

Type of pizza	Frequency	
Pepperoni	12	
Cheese and tomato	24	
Vegetarian	9	
Hawaiian	15	

Draw and label a pie chart to represent this information.

....

....

....

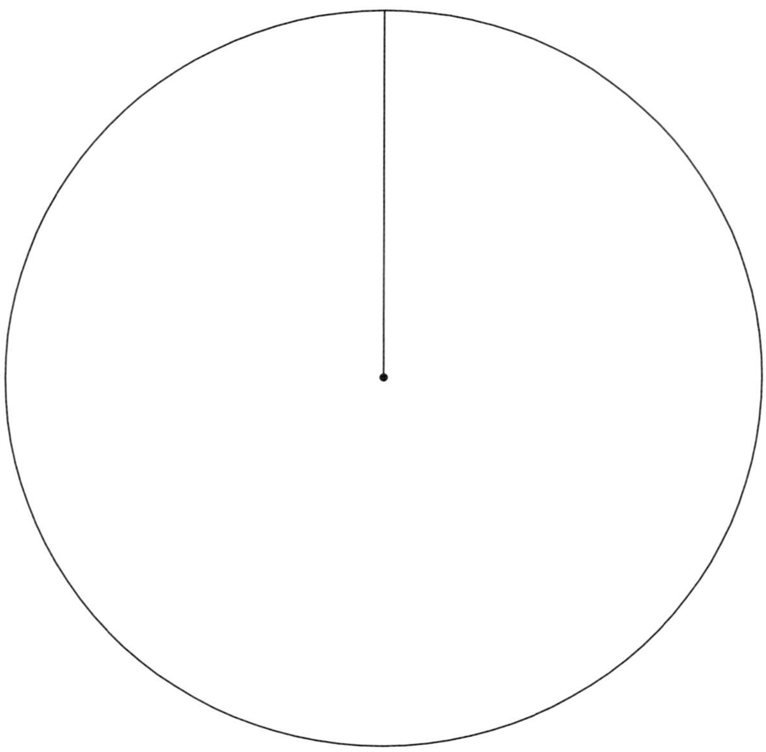

(*4 marks*)

4

LEAVE MARGIN BLANK

6 In his mock examination, Jarad achieved the following percentages for nine different subjects.

56, 73, 68, 60, 65, 53, 76, 56, 64

(a) Construct a stem and leaf diagram to show these numbers.

Key: |.........| ....

....	....
....	....
....	....
....	....

(2 marks)

(b) Write down the median of these numbers.

....

Answer ....% *(1 mark)*

(c) Write down the mode of these numbers.

....

Answer ....% *(1 mark)*

4

LEAVE MARGIN BLANK

7 All pupils in Year 11 in Axton Academy took an aptitude test.
The results for the boys are shown in the cumulative frequency diagram below.

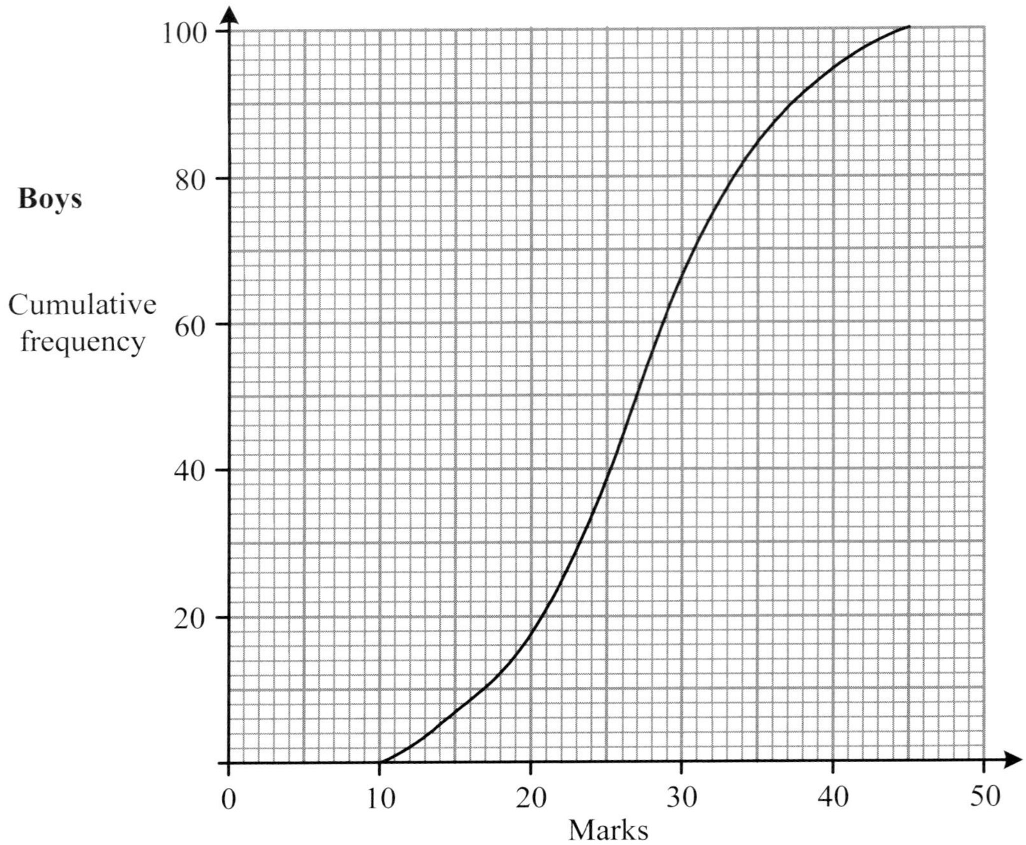

(a) Use the diagram to complete the table below.

Lower quartile	
Median	
Upper quartile	
Interquartile range	
Range	

(3 marks)

The results for the girls are summarised in the box plot below.

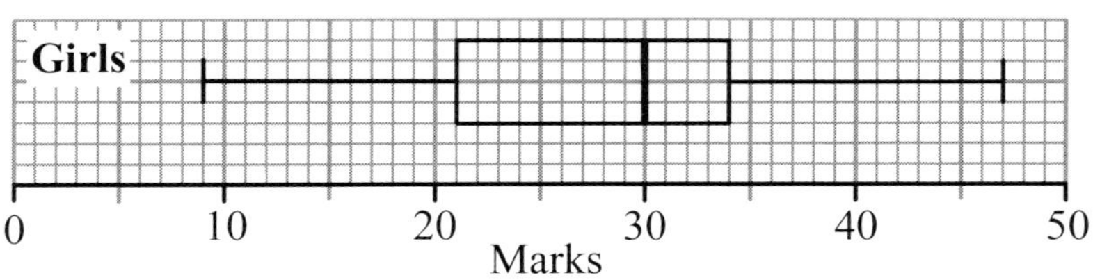

(b) Find the interquartile range for the girls.

....

Answer .... marks *(1 mark)*

THIS QUESTION IS CONTINUED ON THE NEXT PAGE

LEAVE MARGIN BLANK

(c) Describe **two** differences between the distribution for the boys and the distribution for the girls.

....

....

....

(2 marks)

6

8 Victoria keeps a record of the time it takes the school bus to take her from her home to school.
Her record for last month is shown in the table.

Time, *t* minutes	**Frequency**	**Midpoint**
$10 < t \leq 12$	5	
$12 < t \leq 14$	10	
$14 < t \leq 16$	4	
$16 < t \leq 18$	1	

(a) Complete the midpoint column and use it to calculate an estimate of the mean time.

....

....

....

....

Answer .... minutes *(3 marks)*

(b) There are 200 school days in the year.
Use the information in the table to estimate the number of days in a year on which Victoria's bus journey takes more than 14 minutes. (Victoria never misses a day of school!)

....

....

Answer .... *(2 marks)*

(c) What is the probability that, on a randomly chosen day, the journey takes less than 12 minutes?

....

Answer .... *(1 mark)*

6

END OF QUESTIONS

Set 2

MATHEMATICS (MODULAR)
MODULE 3
SECTION A
Time allowed: 40 minutes

In addition to this paper you will require:
- a calculator
- mathematical instruments

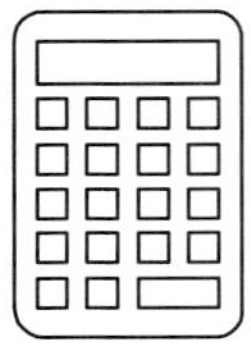

LEAVE MARGIN BLANK

1 In a supermarket, there is a special offer on cans of cola.

The advertisement says, '3 cans of cola for the price of 2.'
The normal price of a can of cola is 36p.

Richard buys 12 cans of cola.

How much does he pay for the cola?

....

....

....

....

Answer £.. *(3 marks)*

3

2 The cost of a camera is £250, plus VAT at 17.5%.

Calculate the amount of VAT charged on the camera.

....

....

....

Answer £.. *(2 marks)*

2

LEAVE MARGIN BLANK

3 An antiques dealer buys a table for £450.
He sells the table for 60% more than the price he paid for it.

(a) For how much does the dealer sell the table?

....

....

....

Answer £.. *(2 marks)*

It costs the dealer £70 to restore the table before he sells it.

(b) Calculate the amount of profit the dealer made.

....

....

....

Answer £.. *(1 mark)*

(c) Calculate this profit as a percentage of the price the dealer paid for the table.

....

....

....

....

Answer ....% *(2 marks)*

5

4 Glenn worked for 4 hours 45 minutes last weekend.

He was paid £4.40 per hour.

How much was Glenn paid last weekend?

....

....

....

....

Answer £.. *(3 marks)*

3

LEAVE MARGIN BLANK

5 (a) Calculate the value of πr^2 when $r = 5.4$.

Give your answer correct to 2 decimal places.

....

....

Answer .... *(2 marks)*

(b) Use your calculator to find the value of

$$\frac{6.86 + 17.35}{8.92 - 5.19}$$

correct to 2 significant figures.

....

....

Answer .... *(2 marks)*

4

6 Jeremy measures the length of his stride.

He records it as 80 cm to the nearest 10 cm.

What is the least possible distance that Jeremy walks when he takes 12 strides?

....

....

....

....

Answer ....cm *(2 marks)*

2

LEAVE MARGIN BLANK

7 (a) Calculate $5.4 \times 10^4 \times 7.2$

Give your answer in standard form.

....

....

....

Answer .... *(2 marks)*

(b) Calculate $5.4 \times 10^4 \div 7.2$

Give your answer in standard form.

....

....

....

Answer .... *(2 marks)*

4

8 Abdul has just been promoted in his job.
When he was promoted, his pay was increased by 25%.

Abdul now earns £6.40 an hour.

How much did he earn per hour before he was promoted?

....

....

....

....

....

Answer £.. *(3 marks)*

3

9 On his 15th birthday in 2000, Shane opened a savings account with £200.

Interest is added to the account every year on Shane's birthday.
Shane is not allowed to withdraw any money from the account until he is 18.

On his 16th birthday, interest of 5.5% is added to his account.

(a) (i) Shane says, 'I can calculate the amount of money in my account by multiplying £200 by 1.055.'

Explain why Shane's method is correct.

....

....

....

....

(2 marks)

(ii) How much is in the account after the interest has been added on Shane's 16th birthday?

....

....

....

Answer £... *(2 marks)*

(b) After Shane's 16th birthday, the bank reduces the rate of interest to 5%.

How much is in the account after the interest has been added on Shane's 18th birthday?

....

....

....

....

....

Answer £... *(2 marks)*

6

END OF SECTION A

Set 2

MATHEMATICS (MODULAR)
MODULE 3
SECTION B
Time allowed: 40 minutes

In addition to this paper you will require:

- mathematical instruments.

You may **not** use a calculator.

LEAVE MARGIN BLANK

10 Work out

(a) 0.4×0.4

....

....

Answer .... (*1 mark*)

(b) $3.05 - 1.47$

....

....

Answer .... (*1 mark*)

2

11 The recommended price of a guitar is £240.

Sanjay discovers that he can order the guitar on the internet and get a discount of 30% off the recommended price.

Calculate the amount Sanjay would pay if he ordered the guitar on the internet.

....

....

....

....

Answer £.. (*3 marks*)

3

LEAVE MARGIN BLANK

12 (a) Which of the following numbers are **not** prime?

2, 5, 9, 11, 17, 27

....

Answer .... (*2 marks*)

(b) Work out $2^6 \div 2^4$

....

....

Answer .... (*2 marks*)

(c) Write 24 out of 400 as a percentage.

....

....

....

Answer .... (*2 marks*)

(d) Write $3\frac{2}{5}$ as a decimal.

....

....

Answer .... (*1 mark*)

(e) Evaluate $\frac{3}{4} + \frac{2}{5}$, giving your answer as a fraction.

....

....

Answer .... (*2 marks*)

9

LEAVE MARGIN BLANK

13 Sid and Alex share a sum of money in the ratio 5:3

Alex receives £16.20.

How much does Sid receive?

....

....

....

....

Answer £.. *(2 marks)*

2

14 Yurika drives 214 miles in 4 hours 53 minutes.

Do a calculation to find an **approximate** value for her average speed.

....

....

....

Answer ....mph *(2 marks)*

Is your approximate value greater or less than Yurika's actual average speed?

Explain your answer.

Answer ....

Reason ....

....

....

(1 mark)

3

LEAVE MARGIN BLANK

15 (a) Express 96 as the product of its prime factors.

....

....

....

....

....

Answer .... (*3 marks*)

(b) What is the highest common factor (HCF) of 18 and 96?

....

....

....

....

Answer .... (*2 marks*)

5

16 (a) Given that $264 \times 37 = 9768$, find the exact value of $\frac{97.68}{2.64}$

....

....

Answer .... (*2 marks*)

(b) Write 579 000 000 000 in standard form.

....

Answer .... (*2 marks*)

4

LEAVE MARGIN BLANK

17 (a) Find an approximate value of $\frac{5.41 \times 61.7}{0.291}$

You **must** show all your working.

....

....

....

Answer .... *(2 marks)*

(b) Andy is investigating recurring decimals.

He is looking at the result of dividing an odd number by the next highest odd number. (for example, dividing 17 by 19).

Andy concludes that the result of dividing an odd number by the next highest odd number is always a recurring decimal.

Show, by means of a counter example, that Andy is **not** correct.

....

....

....

....

(2 marks)

4

END OF QUESTIONS

Set 2

MATHEMATICS (MODULAR)
MODULE 5
Time allowed: 1 hour 15 minutes

In addition to this paper you will require:

- mathematical instruments.

You may **not** use a calculator.

LEAVE MARGIN BLANK

1 Write these fractions in order of size, with the smallest fraction first.

$$\frac{5}{6}, \quad \frac{3}{4}, \quad \frac{7}{9}, \quad \frac{13}{18}$$

....

....

....

Answer .... *(2 marks)*

2

2 *ABCD* is a parallelogram, with angle *ADC* = 65°.

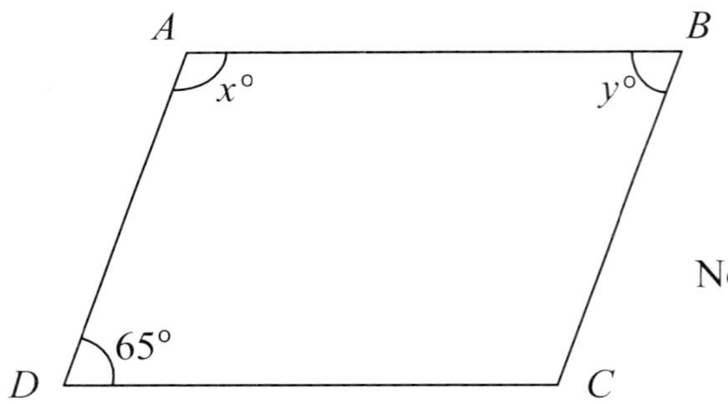

Not to scale

Find the value of x and the value of y.

....

....

....

Answer x = ... degrees

Answer y = ... degrees *(2 marks)*

2

3 The diagram shows a triangular prism.

The cross-section of the prism is a right-angled triangle.

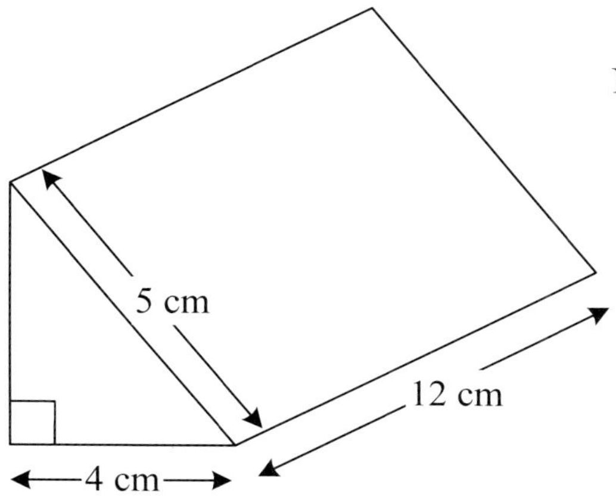

Not to scale

Calculate the volume of the prism.

....

....

....

....

....

....

Answer .... *(6 marks)*

6

4 Marcel walks from home to his friend's house. He stays at his friend's house for a short while and then he runs home.

The graph shows Marcel's journey to and from his friend's house.

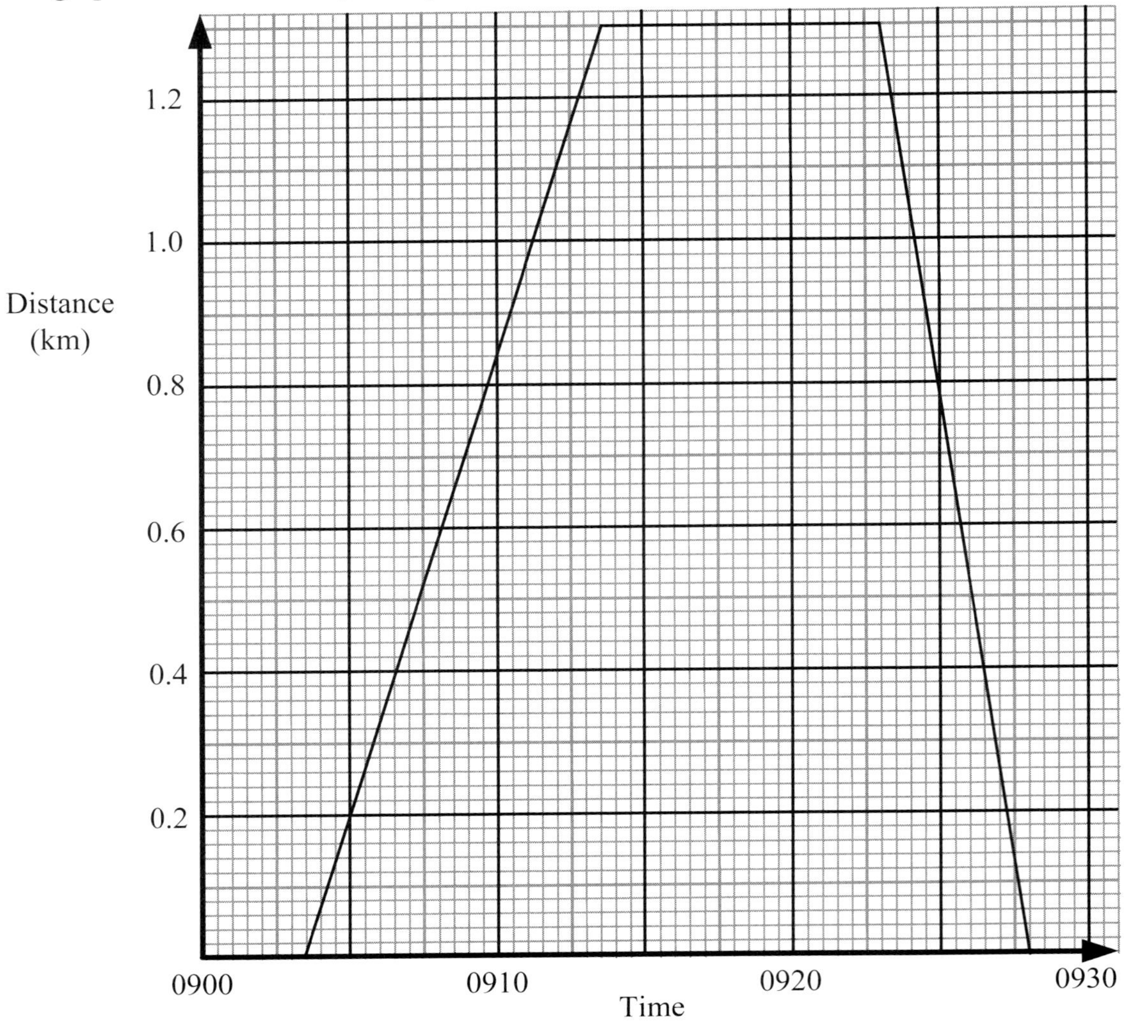

(a) How far is his friend's house from Marcel's home?

....

Answer .... km *(1 mark)*

(b) How long does Marcel stay at his friend's house.

....

Answer .... minutes *(1 mark)*

(c) Calculate, in kilometres per hour, the speed at which Marcel runs home.

....

....

....

Answer .... km/h *(3 marks)*

5

5 The map shows part of a coastline, with a lighthouse and a coastguard station near the coast.

The map is drawn to scale.

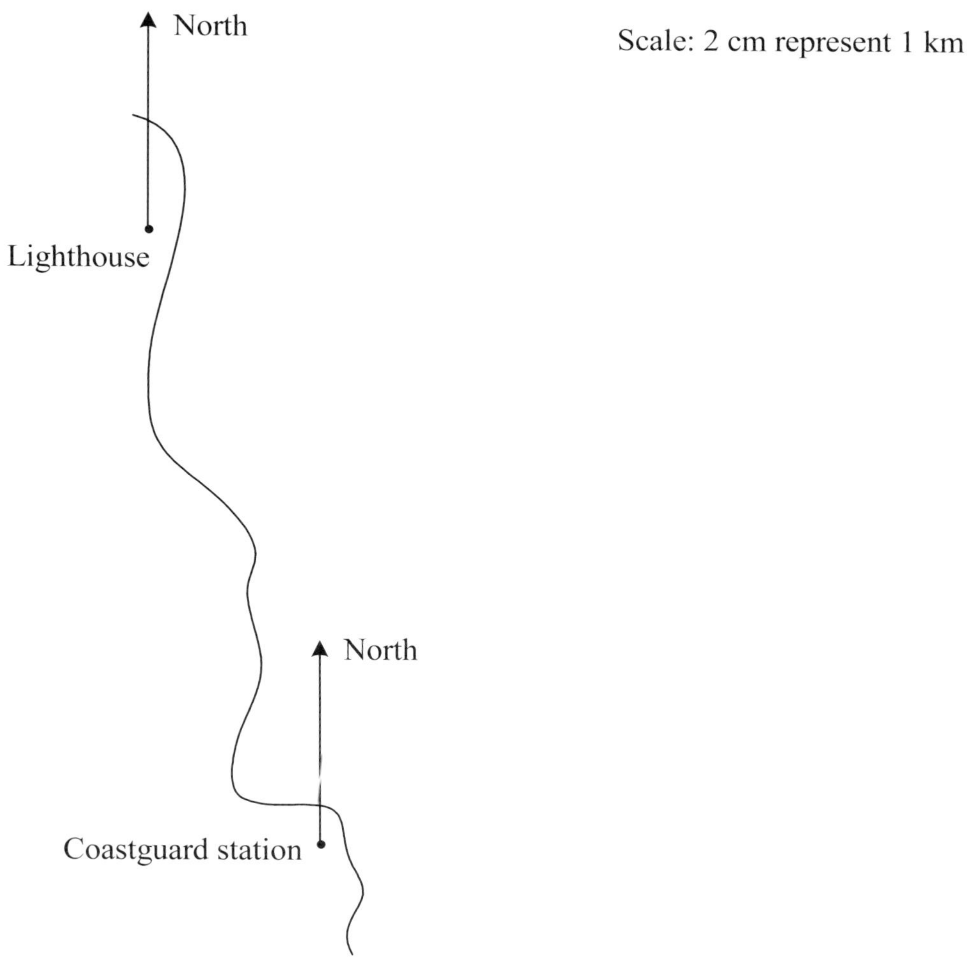

(a) What is the distance, to the nearest 0.1 km, between the lighthouse and the coastguard station?

....

....

Answer ....km *(1 mark)*

An observer in the lighthouse can see a boat at sea. The boat is on a bearing of 132° from the lighthouse.

At the same time, an observer at the coastguard station can see the same boat on a bearing of 065°.

(b) Mark, with a cross, the position of the boat on the diagram.

(2 marks)

3

LEAVE MARGIN BLANK

6 (a) If $a = 4$ and $b = -3$, calculate the value of

$$3a - 2b$$

....

....

Answer .... *(2 marks)*

(b) Solve the equation

$$4x - 5 = 13$$

....

....

....

Answer .... *(2 marks)*

(c) Solve the equation

$$3(x - 4) = 2x - 7$$

....

....

....

....

Answer .... *(2 marks)*

(d) Factorise

$$12 - 6x$$

....

Answer .... *(1 mark)*

7

LEAVE MARGIN BLANK

7 Marie is saving for a holiday.

Each week she saves three tenths of her pay.

Last week Marie saved £54.

How much was she paid last week?

....

....

....

Answer £.. *(3 marks)*

3

8 In the diagram, *A*, *B* and *C* lie on the circumference of the circle, whose centre is *O*. *AD* is a tangent to the circle and *BC* is parallel to *AD*.

Angle *CAD* = 78°.

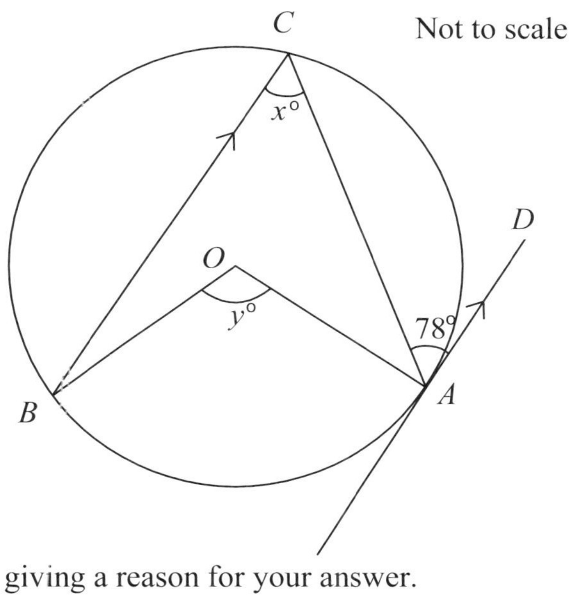

(a) Find the value of *x*, giving a reason for your answer.

....

Answer $x =$ ....° *(1 mark)*

(b) Calculate the value of *y*, giving a reason for your answer.

....

....

....

Answer $y =$ ....° *(2 marks)*

3

LEAVE MARGIN BLANK

9 (a) The diagram shows a triangle *ABC*.

Using a ruler and compasses, construct the perpendicular bisector of *AC*.

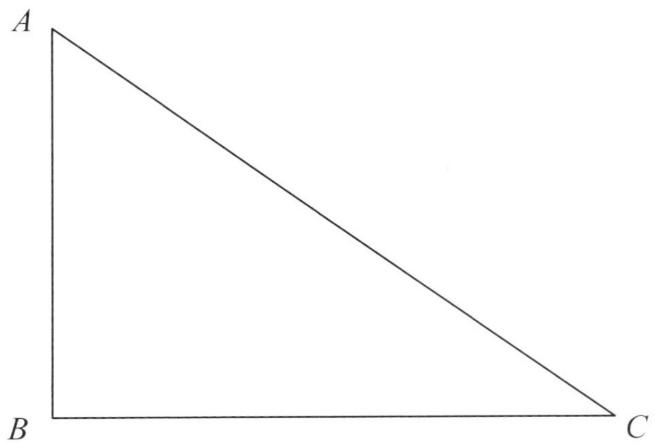

(2 marks)

(b) Triangle *PQR* is an equilateral triangle.

The line *PQ* is drawn below.

Using a ruler and compasses, construct the triangle *PQR*.

(You will get no credit if you do not show all your construction lines.)

(2 marks)

4

LEAVE MARGIN BLANK

10 A rectangle has a length of $(x + 2)$ cm and a width of $(x - 1)$ cm.

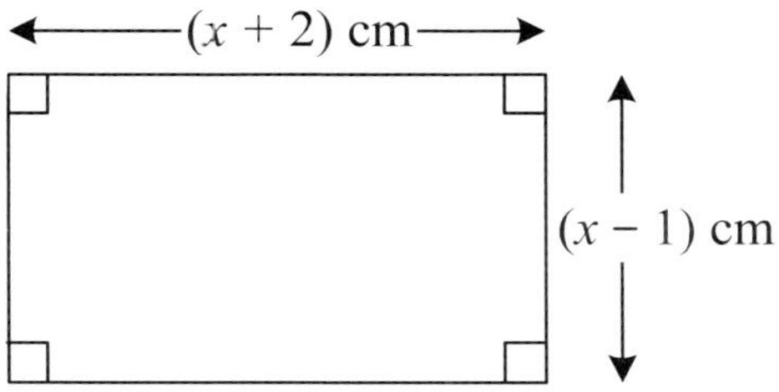

(a) (i) Write down and simplify an expression in terms of x for the perimeter of the rectangle.

....

....

....

Answer .... cm *(2 marks)*

(ii) The perimeter of the rectangle is 26 cm.

Form an equation and solve it to find the value of x.

....

....

....

....

....

Answer .... cm *(2 marks)*

(b) Write down an expression in terms of x for the area of the rectangle.

....

Answer ....cm^2 *(1 mark)*

5

LEAVE MARGIN BLANK

11 (a) Solve the equation

$$x^2 - 3x - 4 = 0$$

....

....

....

....

....

Answer .... *(2 marks)*

(b) Solve the simultaneous equations

$$4x + 3y = 5$$
$$x - 2y = 4$$

....

....

....

....

....

....

....

Answer .... *(2 marks)*

4

12 The diagram below shows a solid.

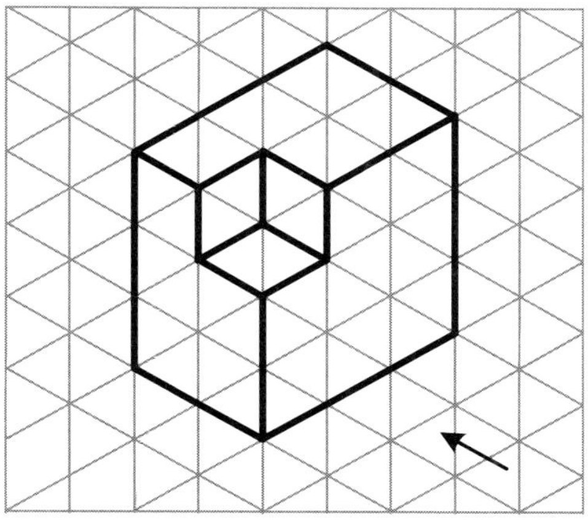

On the grid below, draw the elevation of this solid as seen from the direction of the arrow.

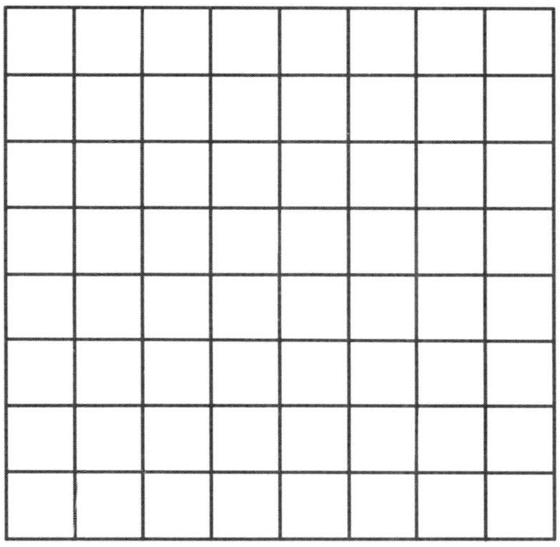

(2 marks)

2

13

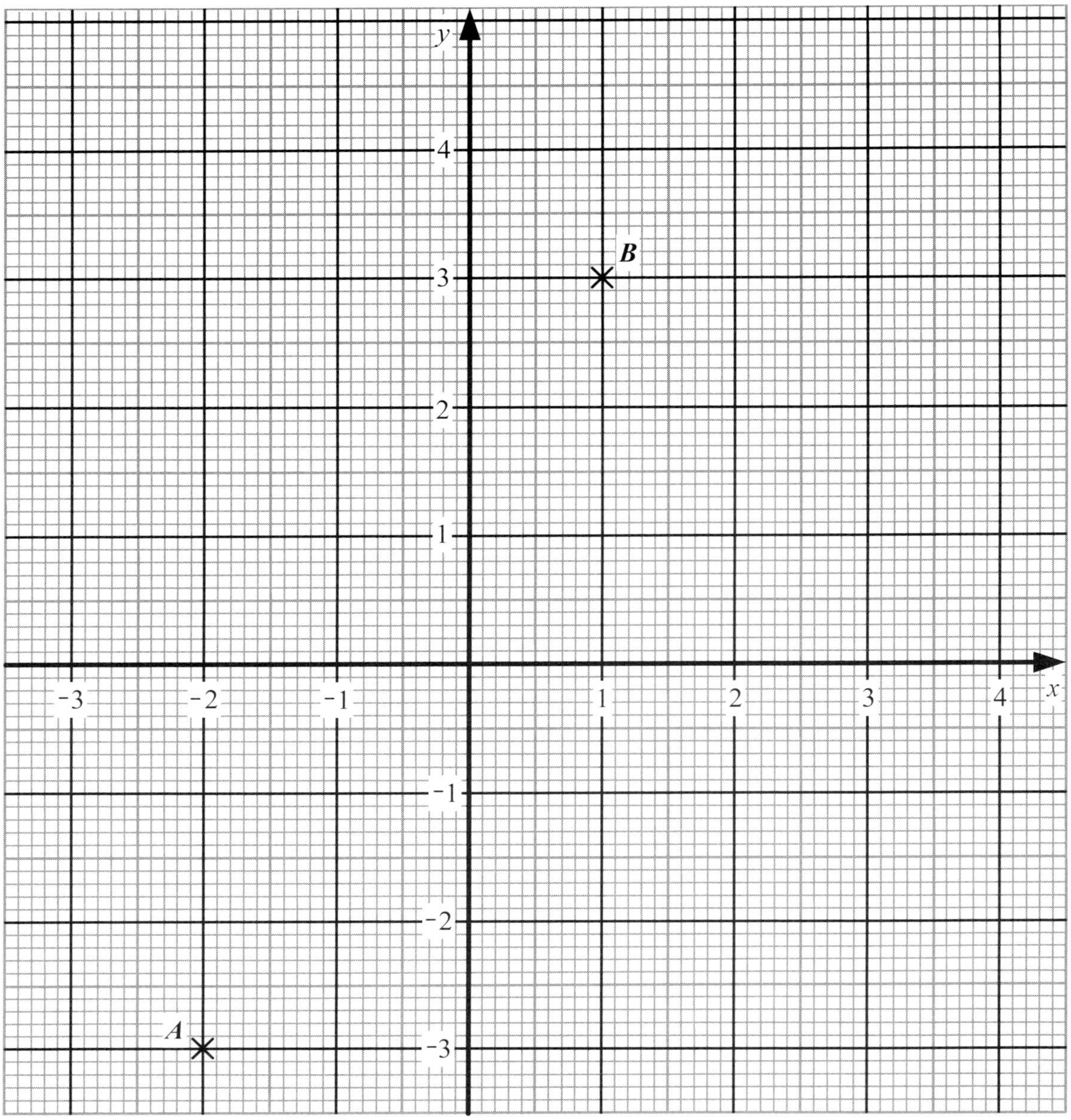

A is the point (–2, –3) and B is the point (1, 3).

(a) Calculate the gradient of the line AB.

....

....

....

Answer .... *(2 marks)*

(b) Write down the coordinates of the mid-point of AB.

....

Answer (.................. , ...) *(1 mark)*

THIS QUESTION IS CONTINUED ON THE NEXT PAGE

(c) Find the equation of the line AB.

....

....

....

Answer .... *(2 marks)*

(d) On the graph, draw the line whose equation is $x + y = 3$, for values of x from -1 to 4 inclusive.

(2 marks)

7

14 (a) Write down the first three terms of the sequence whose nth term is given by $12 - 5n$.

....

....

Answer .... *(2 marks)*

(b) Write down the next two terms of the sequence 64, 32, 16, ..., ...

....

....

Answer .... *(1 mark)*

(c) Miranda has written down the next two terms of the sequence 64, 32, 16, ... , ...

She says, 'The numbers are getting smaller. If I keep going, I will soon find negative numbers in the sequence.'

Is Miranda correct?

Explain your answer.

....

....

....

....

(2 marks)

5

LEAVE MARGIN BLANK

15

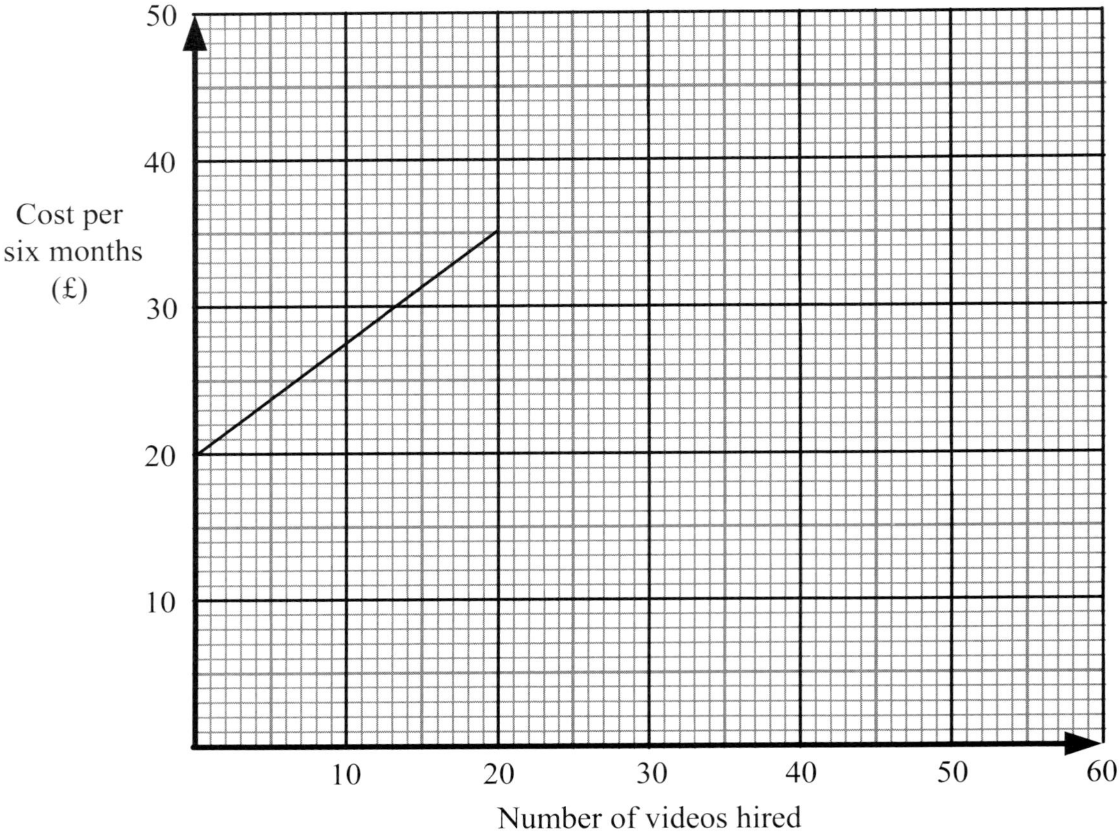

Anna is a member of a video club.

She pays a fixed charge of £20 every six months.

She pays an additional charge for every video she hires.

The line on the graph shows the cost for six months to Anna for up to 20 videos hired.

(a) Calculate the cost of hiring each of the first 20 videos.

....

....

Answer .... pence *(2 marks)*

Once she has hired 20 videos in any six month period, she pays only 50p for every additional video she hires.

(b) Draw a line on the graph so that the graph can be used to calculate the total cost in a six-month period of hiring up to 50 videos.

(3 marks)

5

LEAVE MARGIN BLANK

16 The shape of a solid figure is determined by two lengths, a cm and b cm.

Which one of the following could not be the formula used for working out the volume of the shape?

Give a reason for your answer.

A: $a^2(a+b)$ B: $a(a^2+b^2)$ C: a^3b D: a^2b

Answer ....

Reason ....

....

....

(2 marks)

2

17

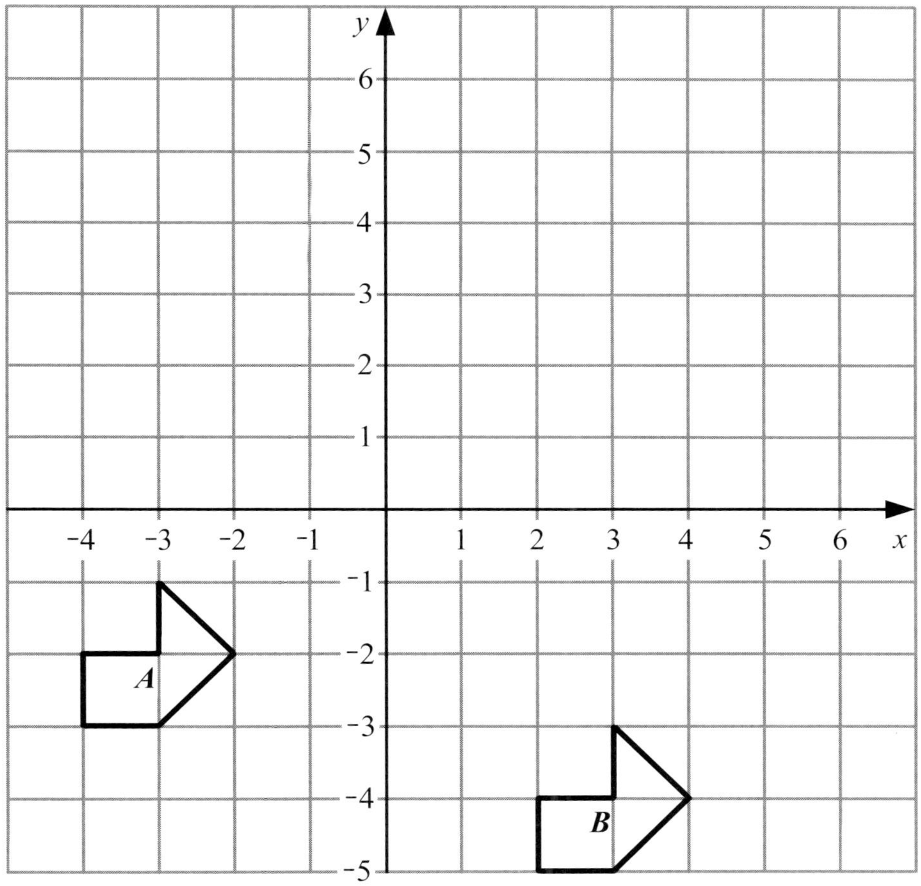

(a) On the graph, draw the finishing position when

(i) Shape A is reflected in the line $y = 1$. *(1 mark)*

(ii) Shape A is rotated through 180° about the point (1, 1) . *(2 marks)*

(b) Describe fully the transformation which will map Shape A onto Shape B. *(2 marks)*

5

END OF QUESTIONS

Set 2

MATHEMATICS (MODULAR)
MODULE 5
Time allowed: 1 hour 15 minutes

In addition to this paper you will require:

- a calculator
- mathematical instruments

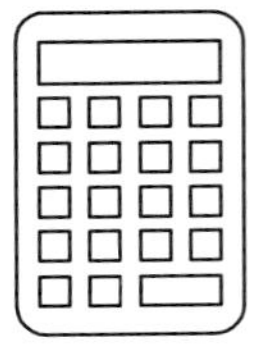

LEAVE MARGIN BLANK

1 The triangle ABC has angles of $3x°$, $4x°$ and $5x°$.

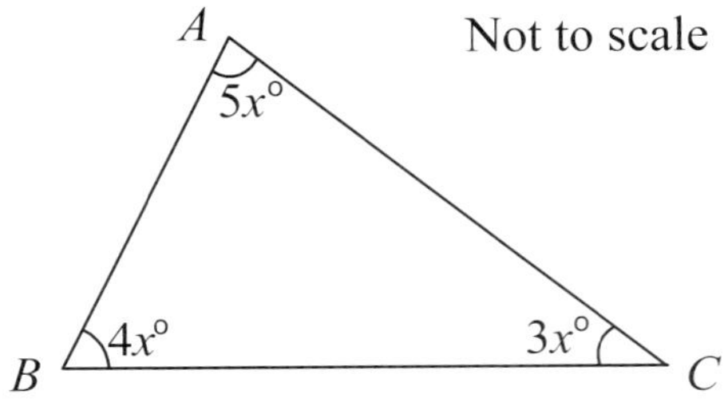

Not to scale

Form an equation and solve it to find the value of x.

....

....

....

....

Answer ....degrees *(3 marks)*

3

2 Marlon says, 'It is not possible to draw a parallelogram that has any axes of symmetry.'

Show, by means of a counter example, that Marlon is wrong.

....

....

....

....

....

(2 marks)

2

LEAVE MARGIN BLANK

3 (a) Find the cube root of 6.3

....

Answer .... *(1 mark)*

(b) Find the value of $\dfrac{6.39 - 2.46}{3.28 \times 0.43}$

....

....

Answer .... *(2 marks)*

(c) If $a = 15$ and $b = -4$, find the value of

(i) $2a + 10b$

....

....

Answer .... *(2 marks)*

(ii) $a \div b$

....

....

Answer .... *(2 marks)*

(iii) $\dfrac{a}{2 + 2b}$

....

....

Answer .... *(2 marks)*

9

LEAVE MARGIN BLANK

4 (a) Make t the subject of the formula $v = u + at$.

....

....

....

Answer t =.. *(2 marks)*

(b) The area of a circle is 24 cm^2.

Find the radius of the circle.

....

....

....

....

....

Answer ....cm *(3 marks)*

5

5 Mushtaq is going to France for his holiday.

He has £65, which he wants to convert to euros.
£1 is worth 1.6 euros.

(a) How many euros does Mushtaq get for £65?

....

....

Answer .... euros *(2 marks)*

Mushtaq returns from holiday with 18 euros, which he exchanges for English currency.

(b) How much does Mushtaq get for his euros?

....

....

Answer £... *(2 marks)*

4

LEAVE MARGIN BLANK

6 The formula used to calculate Jenny's electricity bill is $A = F + 0.08N$.

£A stands for the total amount of the bill. £F represents a fixed charge, and N is the number of units of electricity used.

Calculate the amount of Jenny's bill if the fixed charge is £13.60 and she uses 830 units.

....

....

....

....

Answer £.. *(2 marks)*

2

7 A ladder AB rests on horizontal ground against a vertical wall.

The ladder is 3.8 m long and its end B is 1.2 m from the base of the wall.

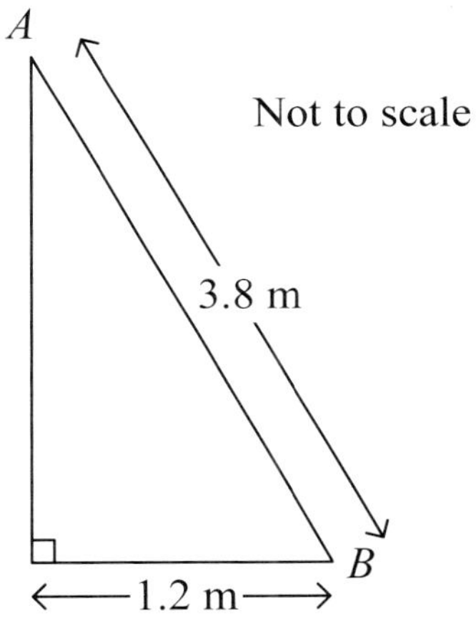

Calculate the angle the ladder makes with the ground.

....

....

....

....

....

....

Answer ....° *(3 marks)*

3

LEAVE MARGIN BLANK

8 Complete the table of values for $y = \frac{1}{x}$ and use it to draw the graph of $y = \frac{1}{x}$ for values of x from $\frac{1}{6}$ to 4.

x	$\frac{1}{6}$	$\frac{1}{4}$	$\frac{1}{2}$	1	2	3	4
y	6			1			$\frac{1}{4}$

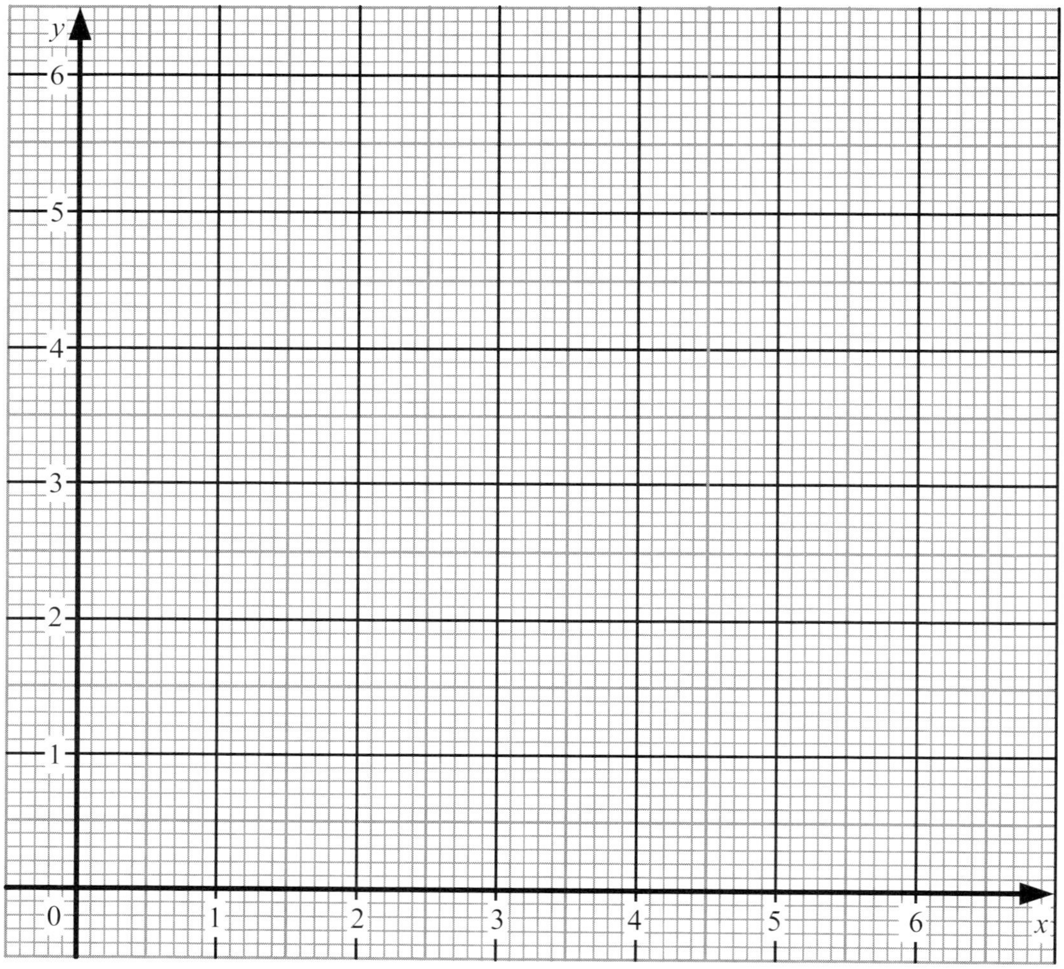

(3 marks)

3

LEAVE MARGIN BLANK

9 Steve is using trial and improvement to find a solution of the equation $x^2 - 3x = 7$.

The table shows his first two trials.

x	$x^2 - 3x$	**Comment**
4	4	Too small
5	10	Too large

Continue the table to find a solution of the equation.

Give your answer correct to **1 decimal place**.

Answer .... *(3 marks)*

3

10 (a) Solve the inequalities

(i) $5x > 3x - 4$

....

....

Answer .... *(2 marks)*

(ii) $6 \leq 10 - 2x$

....

....

Answer .... *(2 marks)*

(b) List all the integers that satisfy both inequalities.

....

Answer .... *(2 marks)*

6

LEAVE MARGIN BLANK

11 In the diagram, $AC = 3.2$ cm, $CD = 4.3$ cm, angle $BAC = 62°$ and angle ACD is a right angle.

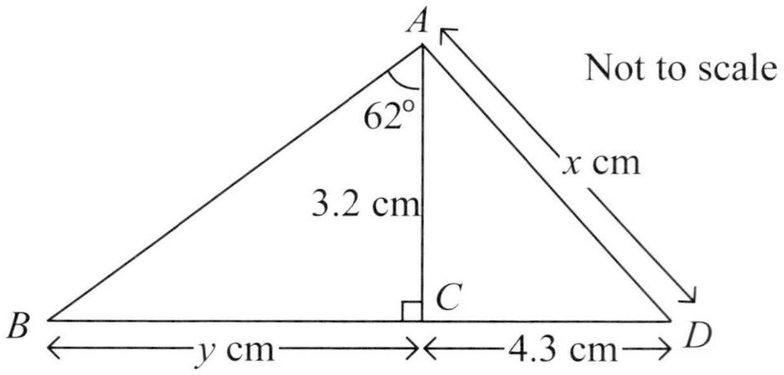

(a) Find the value of x.

....

....

....

....

Answer .... cm *(3 marks)*

(b) Find the value of y.

....

....

....

....

Answer .... cm *(3 marks)*

6

LEAVE MARGIN BLANK

12 Hazel's back garden is in the shape of a trapezium.

In the middle of the garden there is a circular pond of diameter 2 m. The rest of the garden is covered with grass.

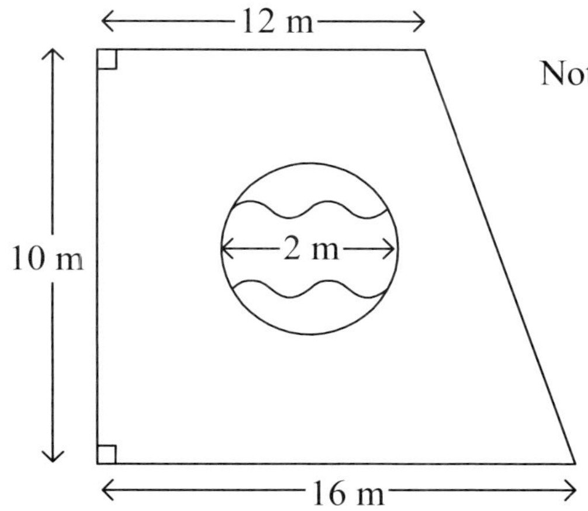

Not to scale

(a) Calculate the area of grass in the garden.

....

....

....

....

....

....

Answer .... m^2 *(4 marks)*

The pond is in the shape of a cylinder. The water in the pond is 60 cm deep.

(b) Calculate, in m^3, the volume of water in the pond.

Give your answer to a suitable degree of accuracy.

....

....

....

....

Answer .... m^3 *(3 marks)*

7

LEAVE MARGIN BLANK

13 (a) Simplify $(x - 3) - (x - 5)$

....

....

Answer .... *(2 marks)*

(b) Solve the equation $\frac{12}{x} = 4$

....

....

Answer .... *(2 marks)*

(c) Multiply out and simplify $(a - 5)^2$

....

....

Answer .... *(2 marks)*

(d) Simplify $4y^3 \times 3y^4$

....

....

Answer .... *(2 marks)*

8

LEAVE MARGIN BLANK

14 Faith has a patio in the shape of a rectangle.
She knows that, to the nearest metre, the patio is 10 m long and 4 m wide.

(a) Write down the least possible length and the greatest possible width of the patio.

Least length .... m

Greatest width ....m *(2 marks)*

(b) Faith buys square paving slabs to cover the patio.
The sides of each slab are 50 cm long, measured to the nearest cm.

What is the least possible length of 20 of these slabs laid side by side?

....

....

....

....

....

Answer .... cm *(2 marks)*

4

15 Factorise $x^2 - 9$

....

....

Answer .... *(2 marks)*

2

LEAVE MARGIN BLANK

16 On the grid below indicate clearly the region *R* defined by the three inequalities

$$x \le 2$$

$$y \le x + 3$$

$$x + y \ge -3$$

Mark the region clearly with an *R*.

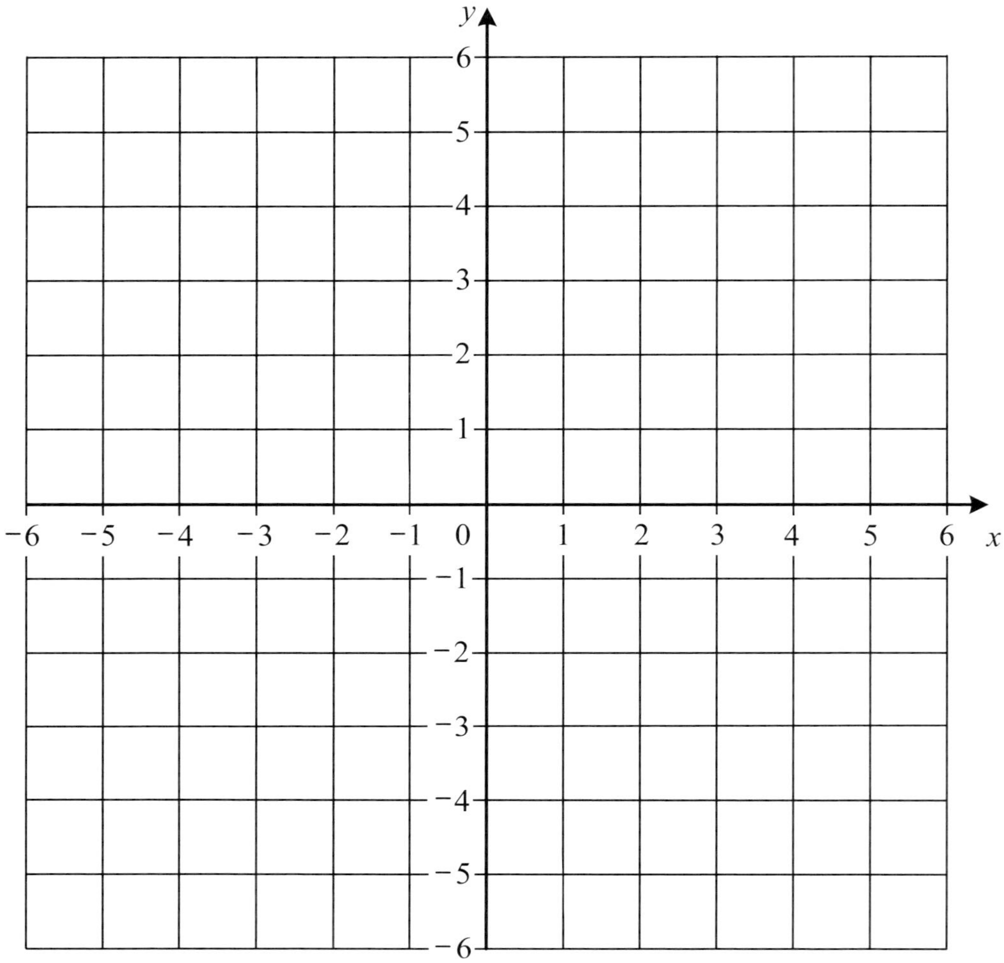

(3 marks)

3

END OF QUESTIONS

Set 1: Module 1 A

1 (a)

		Card in red bag		
		1	3	5
Card in green bag	2	3	5	7
	4	5	7	9
	6	7	9	11

(b) $\frac{1}{9}$ (c) $\frac{2}{3}$

2 $\frac{133}{200}$

3 (a) *Either* bar chart *or* frequency polygon

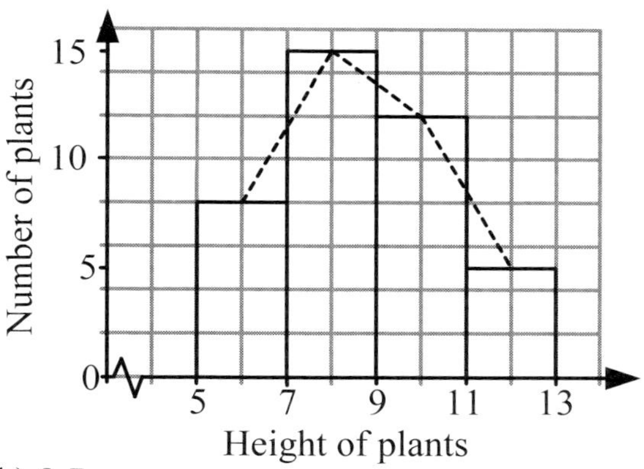

(b) 8.7 cm

4 (a)

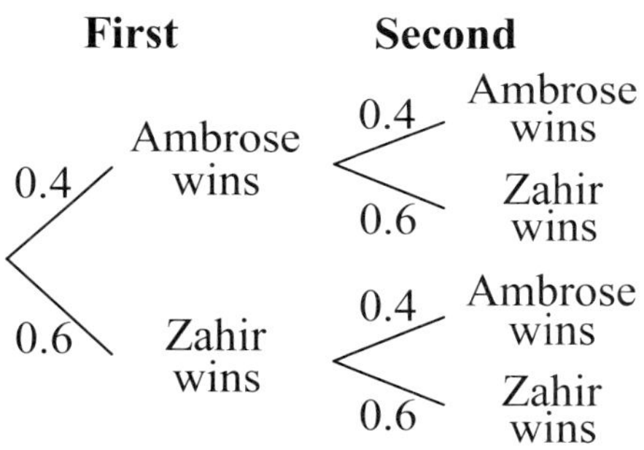

(b) 0.48 (c) 0.16

Set 1: Module 1 B

5 (a) 6 pupils (b) 23 laps (c) 23.5 laps

6 (a) 1.6 litres

(b)

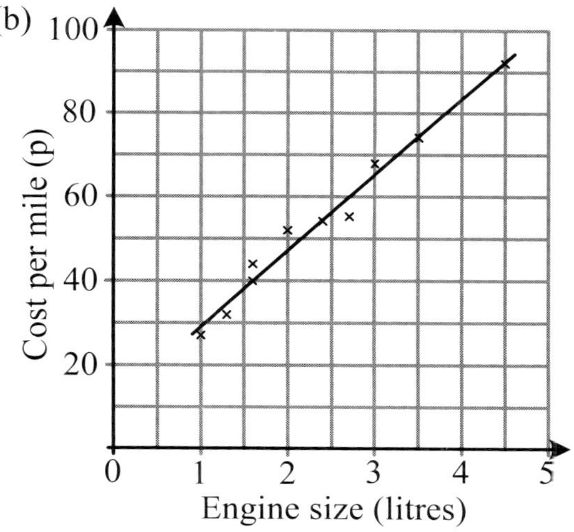

(c) Positive correlation (d) (i) ≈20p
(ii) Possibly not reliable – outside the range covered by the line of best fit.

7 (a)

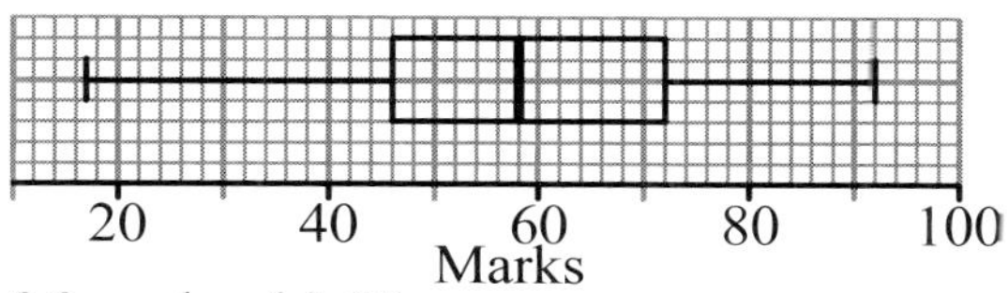

(b) 26 marks (c) 90

(d)

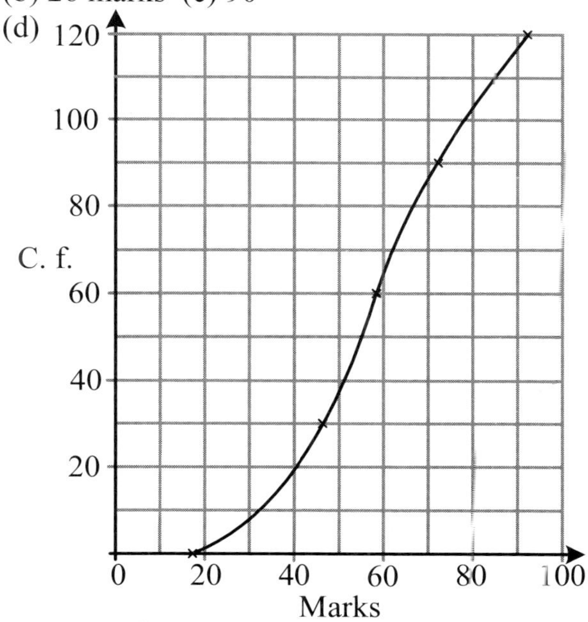

(e) 44 pupils

Set 1: Module 3 A

1 14 km/h

2 55.7% or 56%

3 (a) 135 (b) £432.50 (c) 73%

4 (a) 27 (b) 13 (c) 16

5 £28.95

6 2.59

7 £20

8 (a) 2.998×10^5 km/s (b) $1.798\,8 \times 10^7$ km

9 1977 ml

10 £175

Set 1: Module 3 B

11 Not true for two even squares or two odd squares.

12 (a) £6.75 (b) £60.75

13 (a) 31, 37 (b) 24 (c) 0.06 (d) $\frac{1}{12}$

14 £8.75

15 (a) 150 (b) Standard bar

16 2×3^3 or $2 \times 3 \times 3 \times 3$

17 (a) $\times 10^{-2}$ for correct answer (b) 10.032

18 (a) 27-30 (b) e.g. 6×10^7

Set 1: Module 5, non-calculator

1 0.6, 0.607, $\frac{5}{8}$, $\frac{2}{3}$

2 54°. Angles in triangle total 180°.

3 (a) 36 000 cm^3 (b) 24 000 cm^3

4 (a) 3 (b) 27

5 (a) 033° (b) 315°

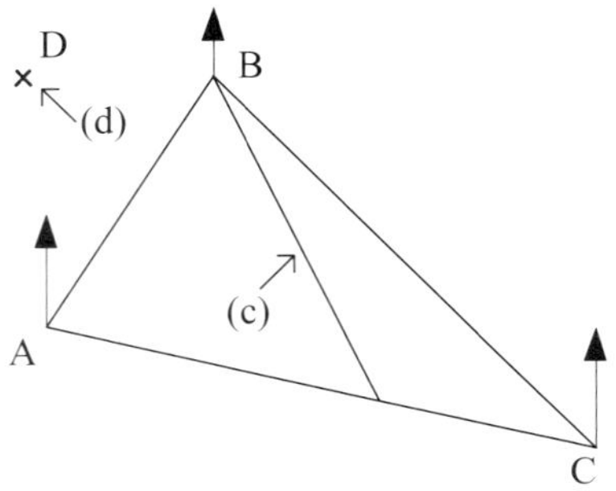

6 (a) 16 km (b) 45 (c) 80 km/h

7 84 cm^2

8 (a) 4, 7, 12 (b) 403 (c) $n^2 + 5$

9

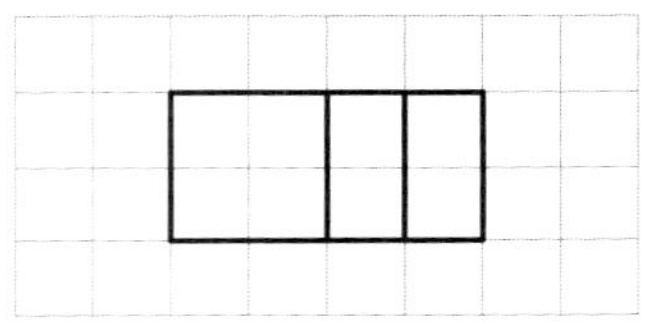

10 (a) $x(x - 3)$ (b) $x = 3\frac{1}{3}$ (c) $x = 22$

11 (a) – 9, 7

(b)

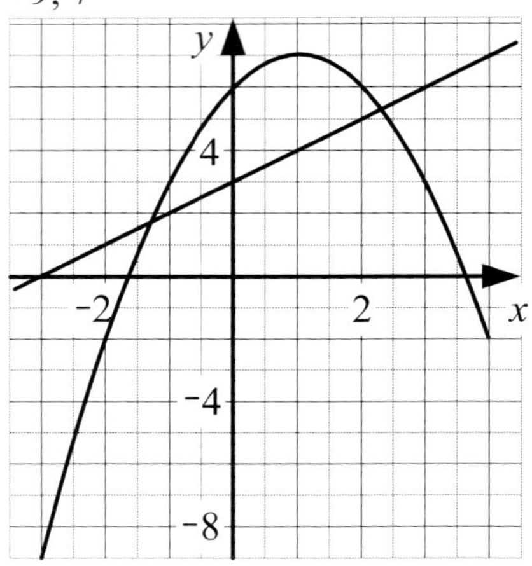

(c) (2.3, 5.3)

12 (a) (10, 4)
(b)

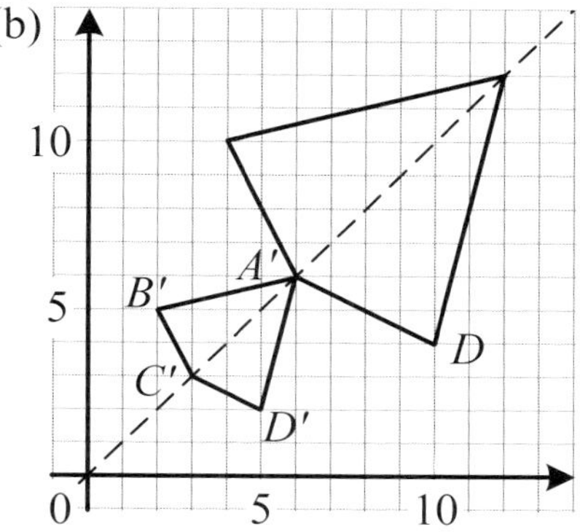

13

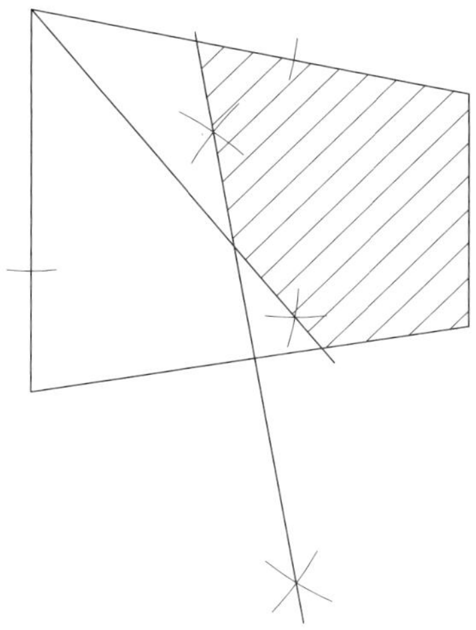

14 (a) 73°; $AO = CO$ (b) 17°; $\angle ACB = 90°$

15 Not correct. Dimensions give cm^2.

16 (a) 3, 4, 1 (b)

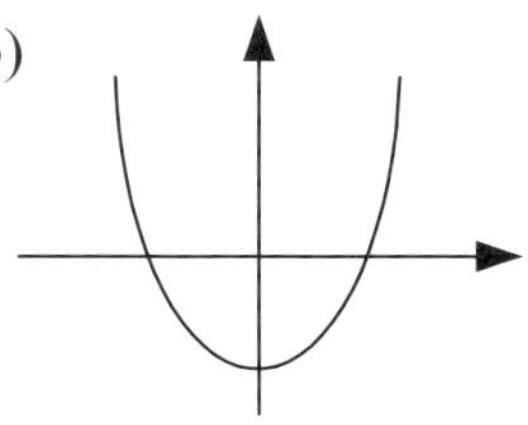

17 (a) (i) $(x - 2)(x - 3)$ (ii) $x = 2, 3$
(b) $x = 5, y = -2$

Set 1: Module 5, calculator

1 (a) (i) 6, (ii) 60° (b) 27°

2 (a) (i) $2n - 3$ (ii) $2(n - 3)$ (iii) $n^2 - 3$
(b) e.g. Garfunkel starts with n marbles. He gives 3 marbles away. He then loses half the number he has left. Garfunkel now has $\frac{n-3}{2}$ marbles.

3 (a) $x > -3$ (b) $2x^2 + 5x - 3$ (c) $6x^6$
(d) $\frac{x^2}{3}$

4 3.6

5 (a) $x = 3\frac{1}{2}$ (b) $Q = \dfrac{S + P}{2}$

6 (a) 1.875 (b) (i) –4, (ii) 160, (iii) $\frac{3}{10}$

7 (a) 2.4 cm (b) 62.5°

8 (a)

$n - 1$	n	$n + 1$
	$n + 10$	
	$n + 20$	

(b) $5n + 30$ (c) Not divisible by 5

9 (a) 80 min (b) 2.25 kg
(c) $T = 40W + 20$

10

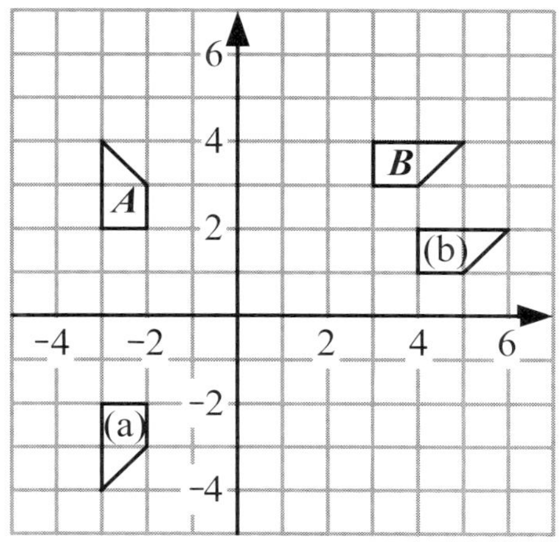

(c) Rotation 90° clockwise about (1, 0)

11 (a) Area of bottom = πr^2; curved surface area = $2\pi rh$ (b) 217 cm^2

12 (a) 23.5 cm (b) 23.75 cm (c) Yes. Least possible length of Asif's foot is less than greatest possible length of Bashir's foot.

13 (a)
(b)

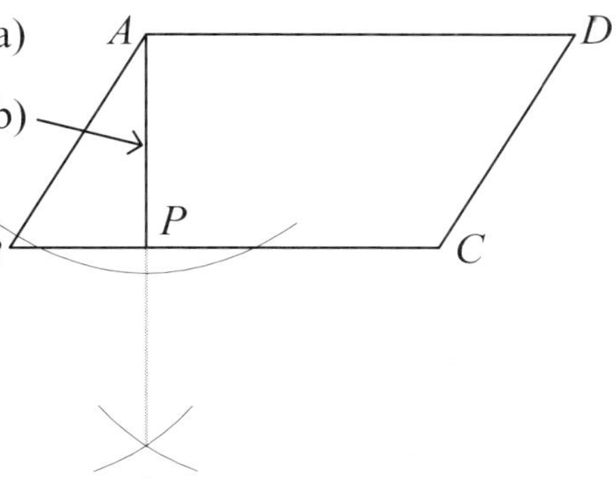

(c) 50 cm^2

Set 2: Module 1 A

1 (a)

		Blue spinner			
		0	1	2	4
	0	0	0	0	0
Yellow spinner	1	0	1	2	4
	2	0	2	4	8
	4	0	4	8	16

(b) $\frac{1}{16}$ (c) $\frac{3}{16}$

2 (a) 0.1 (b) 0.3

3 (a) 1200 children (b) Survey conducted at swimming pool – possible bias towards swimmers.

4 (a) 100
(b) 200

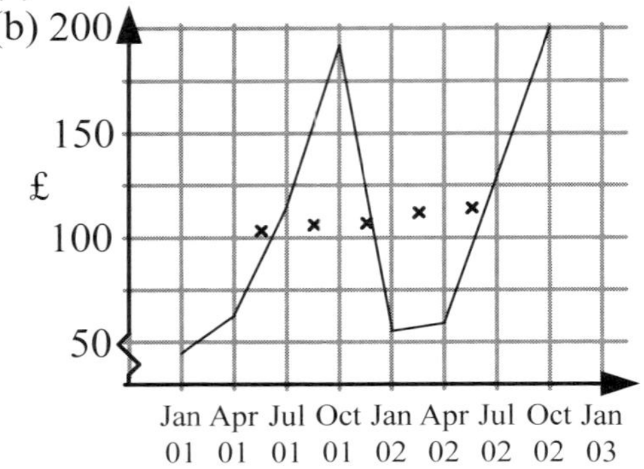

(c) £114 (d) £66

Set 2: Module 1 B

5

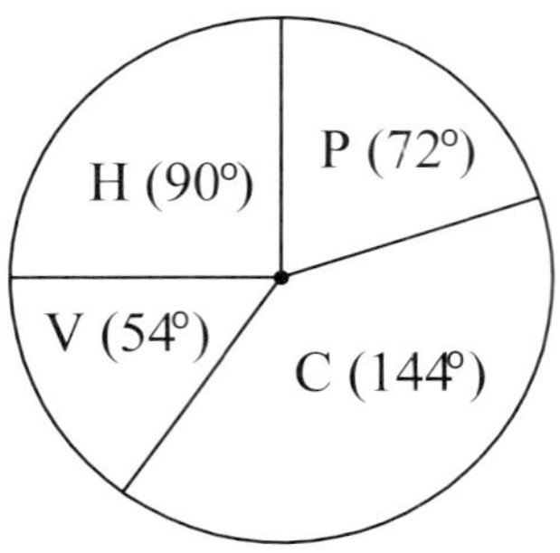

6 (a)

5	3 6 6
6	0 4 5 8
7	3 6

(b) 64
(c) 56

7 (a)

Lower quartile	22
Median	27
Upper quartile	32
Interquartile range	10
Range	35

(b) 13 marks (c) Girls: median higher, iqr higher, range slightly higher

8 (a) 11, 13, 15, 17; 13.1 min (b) 50 days (c) 0.25

Set 2: Module 3 A

1 £2.88

2 £43.75

3 (a) £720 (b) £200 (c) 44.4%

4 £20.90

5 (a) 91.61 (b) 6.5

6 900 cm

7 (a) 3.888×10^5 (b) 7.5×10^3

8 £5.12

9 (a) (ii) £211 (b) £232.63

Set 2: Module 3 B

10 (a) 0.16 (b) 1.58

11 £168

12 (a) 9, 27 (b) 4 (c) 6% (d) 3.4 (e) $1\frac{3}{20}$

13 £27.00

14 ≈ 40 mph. Less: rounding 214 miles down and 4 h 53 min up both make the approximation smaller than the actual number.

15 (a) $2^5 \times 3$ (b) 6

16 (a) 37 (b) 5.79×10^{11}

17 (a) ≈ 1000 (b) Not correct for e.g. 3 ÷ 5

Set 2: Module 5, non-calculator

1 $\frac{13}{18}, \frac{3}{4}, \frac{7}{9}, \frac{5}{6}$

2 $x = 115°, y = 65°$

3 72 cm^3

4 (a) 1.3 km (b) 9.5 min (c) 15.6 km/h

5 (a) 4.4 km
(b)

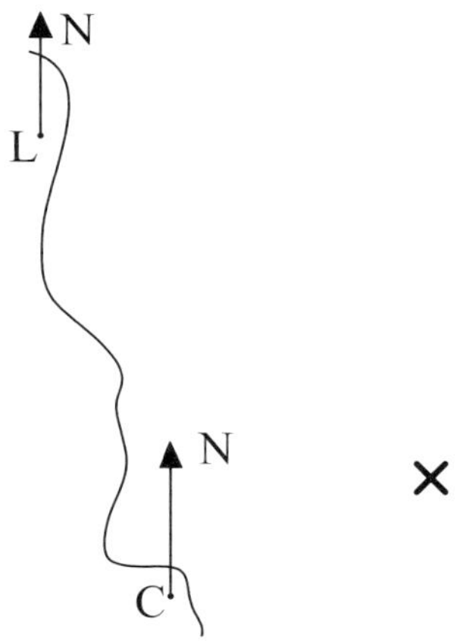

6 (a) 18 (b) $x = 4\frac{1}{2}$ (c) $x = 5$ (d) $6(2 - x)$

7 £180

8 (a) 78°; alternate angles (b) 156°; twice angle at circumference

9 (a)

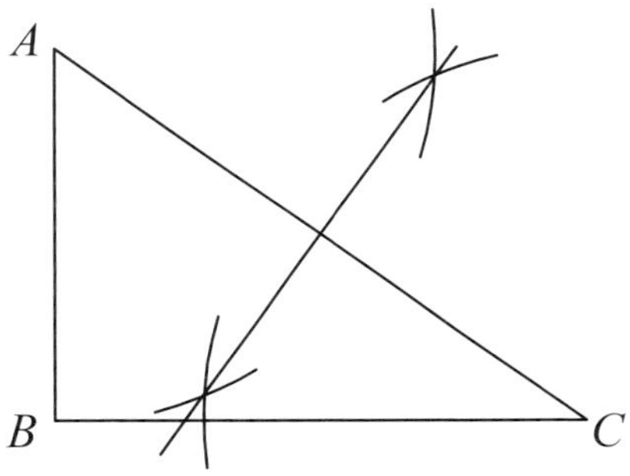

(b)

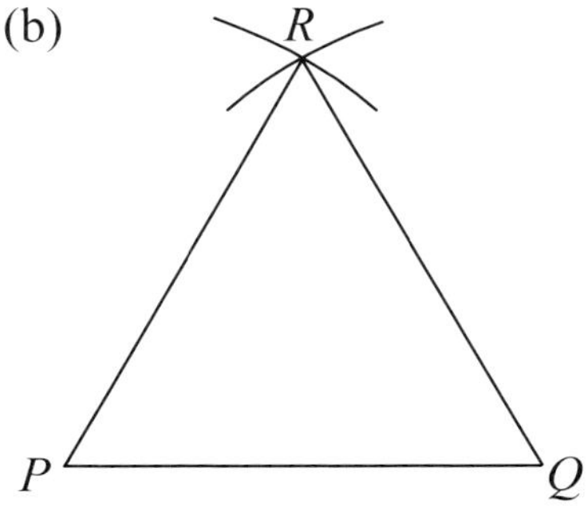

10 (a) (i) $4x + 2$ cm (ii) $x = 6$
(b) $(x + 2)(x - 1)$ cm^2

11 (a) $x = -1, 4$ (b) $x = 2, y = -1$

12

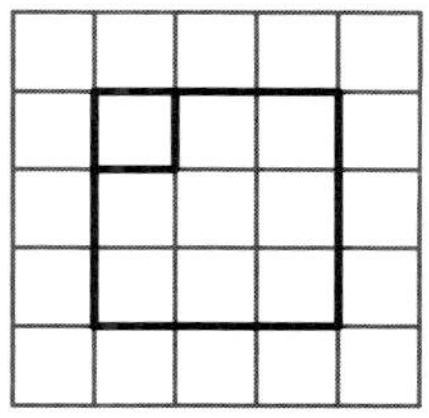

13 (a) 2 (b) $(-\frac{1}{2}, 0)$ (c) $y = 2x + 1$
(d)

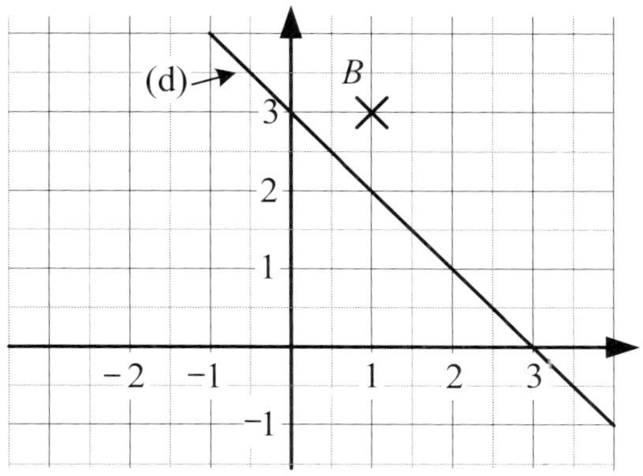

14 (a) 7, 2, –3 (b) 8, 4 (c) Not correct; dividing a positive number by 2 always gives a positive result.

15 (a) 75p
(b)

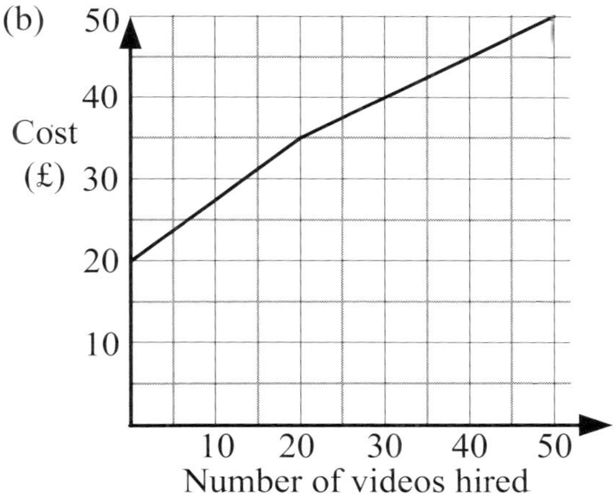

16 C; dimensions give cm^4.

17 (a)

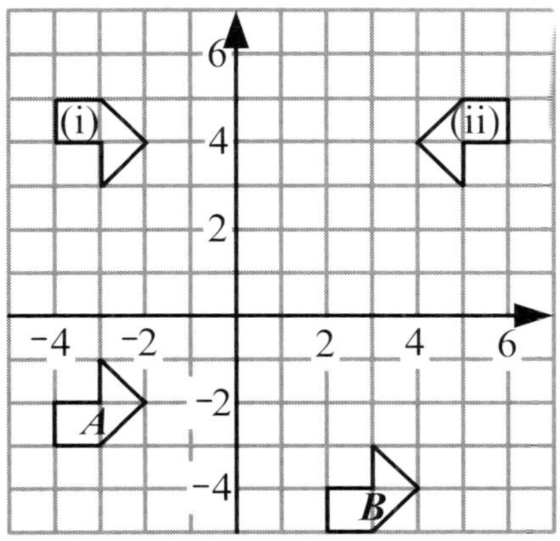

(b) Translation by $\begin{pmatrix} 6 \\ -2 \end{pmatrix}$

Set 2: Module 5, calculator

1 $x = 15°$

2 Rhombus, rectangle, square

3 (a) 1.85 (3 s.f.) (b) 2.79 (c) (i) –10 (ii) –3.75 (iii) –2.5

4 (a) $t = \frac{v - u}{a}$ (b) 2.76 cm

5 (a) 104 euros (b) £11.25

6 £80

7 71.6°

8 (a)

x	$\frac{1}{6}$	$\frac{1}{4}$	$\frac{1}{2}$	1	2	3	4
y	6	4	2	1	$\frac{1}{2}$	$\frac{1}{3}$	$\frac{1}{4}$

(b)

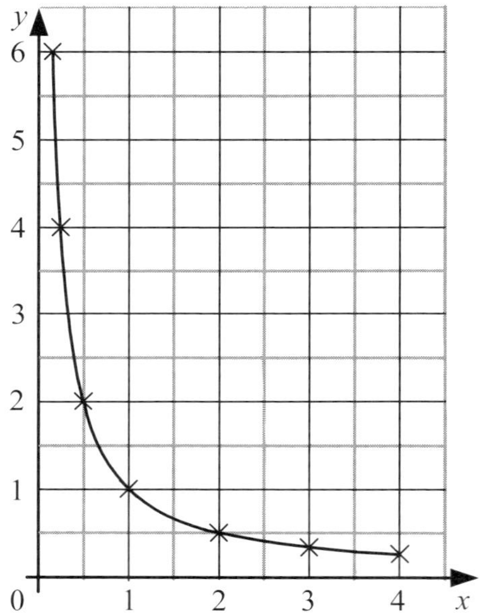

9 4.5

10 (a) (i) $x > -2$ (ii) $x \leq 2$ (b) –1, 0, 1, 2

11 (a) 5.36 cm (b) 6.02

12 (a) 137 m^2 (b) 1.9 m^3

13 (a) 2 (b) $x = 3$ (c) $a^2 - 10a + 25$ (d) $12y^7$

14 (a) 9.5 m, 4.5 m (b) 990 cm

15 $(x - 3)(x + 3)$

16

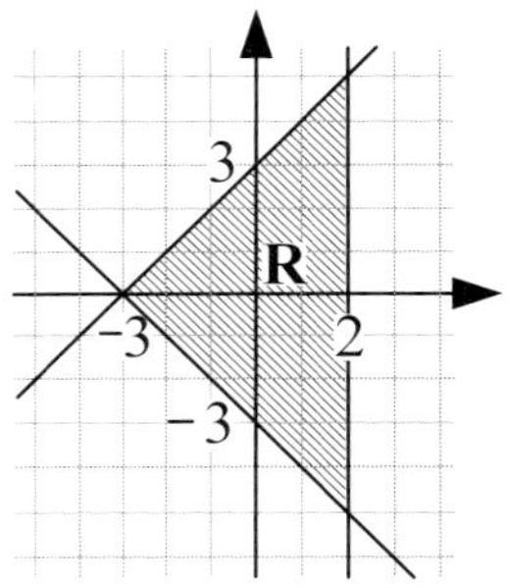

Order Form

Firm Orders – please add quantity required in 'Order Qty' column.
Teachers only: To obtain an Approval Copy please tick the relevant 'A' box(es). Where a tick box is shaded this option is not available.

Coursework Guidance and AQA Module Books

Order Qty	A		ISBN	Title	Order Value*
______	☐	(1)	0 582 79599 0	GCSE Maths Coursework Companion	________
______	☐	(2)	0 582 79593 1	AQA GCSE Maths Intermediate Module 1	________
______	☐	(3)	0 582 79594 X	AQA GCSE Maths Intermediate Module 3	________
______	☐	(4)	0 582 79595 8	AQA GCSE Maths Intermediate Module 5	________
______	☐	(5)	0 582 79596 6	AQA GCSE Maths Higher Module 1	________
______	☐	(6)	0 582 79597 4	AQA GCSE Maths Higher Module 3	________
______	☐	(7)	0 582 79598 2	AQA GCSE Maths Higher Module 5	________

GCSE Maths Exam Tutor

Order Qty	A		ISBN	Title	Order Value*
______	☐	(8)	0 582 82262 9	GCSE Maths Tutor Intermediate Workbook & CD ROM	________
______	☐	(9)	0 582 82264 5	GCSE Maths Tutor Higher Workbook & CD ROM	________
______	(shaded)	(10)	0 582 82789 2	GCSE Maths Tutor Intermediate Site License	________
______	(shaded)	(11)	0 582 82788 4	GCSE Maths Tutor Higher Site License	________

***Call 0800 579 579 or visit www.longman.co.uk to check the price of each component**

TOTAL ORDER VALUE

YOUR DETAILS (Please use BLOCK capitals)

Mr/Mrs/Miss/Ms/Dr ____________________
School ____________________
____
Position ____________________
Address ____________________
____
Postcode ____________________
Telephone No ____________________

REFERENCE CODE ED03-132 (Please quote when ordering)

Choose the most convenient way to pay:

❑ I enclose a cheque for £ __________
made payable to *Pearson Education Limited.*

❑ **Teachers only:** please invoice me
My school order number is ____________.

FOR CREDIT CARD ORDERS, please call our Schools Enquiry Line FREE on 0800 579 579, Reference Code ED03-132.

Signature____________________ Date__________

To receive your FREE e-newsletter containing the latest information on free resources and special offers please register at www.longman.co.uk

Complete and return this form or a photocopy to our FREEPOST address: Secondary Marketing Department, Schools Division, Longman, FREEPOST ANG2041, HARLOW, Essex, CM20 2YF. No stamp required if posted in the UK.
Alternatively phone FREE on 0800 579 579 quoting Reference Code ED03-132.

SINGLE USER LICENCE AGREEMENT FOR GCSE MATHS EXAM TUTOR: INTERMEDIATE TIER

IMPORTANT: READ CAREFULLY

WARNING: BY OPENING THE PACKAGE YOU AGREE TO BE BOUND BY THE TERMS OF THE LICENCE AGREEMENT BELOW.

This is a legally binding agreement between You (the user or purchaser) and Pearson Education Limited. By retaining this licence, any software media or accompanying written materials or carrying out any of the permitted activities You agree to be bound by the terms of the licence agreement below.

If You do not agree to these terms then promptly return the entire publication (this licence and all software, written materials, packaging and any other components received with it) with Your sales receipt to Your supplier for a full refund.

YOU ARE PERMITTED TO:

- Use (load into temporary memory or permanent storage) a single copy of the software on only one computer at a time. If this computer is linked to a network then the software may only be installed in a manner such that it is not accessible to other machines on the network.
- Make one copy of the software solely for backup purposes or copy it to a single hard disk, provided you keep the original solely for back up purposes.
- Transfer the software from one computer to another provided that you only use it on one computer at a time.
- Print a single copy of any PDF file from the CD-ROM for the sole use of the user.

YOU MAY NOT:

- Rent or lease the software or any part of the publication.
- Copy any part of the documentation, except where specifically indicated otherwise.
- Make copies of the software, other than for backup purposes.
- Reverse engineer, decompile or disassemble the software.
- Use the software on more than one computer at a time.
- Install the software on any networked computer in a way that could allow access to it from more than one machine on the network.
- Use the software in any way not specified above without the prior written consent of Pearson Education Limited.
- Print off multiple copies of any PDF file.

ONE COPY ONLY

This licence is for a single user copy of the software

PEARSON EDUCATION LIMITED RESERVES THE RIGHT TO TERMINATE THIS LICENCE BY WRITTEN NOTICE AND TO TAKE ACTION TO RECOVER ANY DAMAGES SUFFERED BY PEARSON EDUCATION LIMITED IF YOU BREACH ANY PROVISION OF THIS AGREEMENT.

Pearson Education Limited owns the software. You only own the disk on which the software is supplied.

Pearson Education Limited warrants that the diskette or CD-ROM on which the software is supplied are free from defects in materials and workmanship under normal use for ninety (90) days from the date You receive them. This warranty is limited to You and is not transferable. Pearson Education Limited does not warrant that the functions of the software meet Your requirements or that the media is compatible with any computer system on which it is used or that the operation of the software will be unlimited or error free.

You assume responsibility for selecting the software to achieve Your intended results and for the installation of, the use of and the results obtained from the software. The entire liability of Pearson Education Limited and its suppliers and your only remedy shall be replacement of the components that do not meet this warranty free of charge.

This limited warranty is void if any damage has resulted from accident, abuse, misapplication, service or modification by someone other than Pearson Education Limited. In no event shall Pearson Education Limited or its suppliers be liable for any damages whatsoever arising out of installation of the software, even if advised of the possibility of such damages. Pearson Education Limited will not be liable for any loss or damage of any nature suffered by any party as a result of reliance upon or reproduction of or any errors in the content of the publication.

Pearson Education Limited does not limit its liability for death or personal injury caused by its negligence.

This licence agreement shall be governed by and interpreted and construed in accordance with English law.

Details of how to purchase a Multiple User Site Licence are given on page 95.